GREAT MINDS

GREAT MINDS

Encounters with Social Theory

GIANFRANCO POGGI AND
GIUSEPPE SCIORTINO

STANFORD SOCIAL SCIENCES

An Imprint of Stanford University Press

Stanford, California

Stanford University Press
Stanford, California

Printed in the United States of America on acid-free, archival-quality paper

Library of Congress Cataloging-in-Publication Data

Poggi, Gianfranco, 1934- author.
 [Incontri con il pensiero sociologico. English]
 Great minds : encounters with social theory / Gianfranco Poggi and Giuseppe Sciortino.
   pages cm
 Translation of: Incontri con il pensiero sociologico.
 Includes bibliographical references and index.
 ISBN 978-0-8047-7213-6 (cloth : alk. paper) — ISBN 978-0-8047-7214-3 (pbk. : alk. paper)
 1. Sociology—History. 2. Sociologists—History. I. Sciortino, Giuseppe, 1963- author. II. Title.
 HM435.P6413 2011
 301.092'2—dc22

                          2010047310

Typeset by Bruce Lundquist in 10/15 Minion

To Marcella and Martina

CONTENTS

Introduction   1

1   Karl Marx   7

2   Emile Durkheim   27

3   Max Weber   49

4   Georg Simmel   71

5   George Herbert Mead   91

6   Talcott Parsons   105

7   Erving Goffman   121

8   Harold Garfinkel   137

9   Niklas Luhmann   155

Other Ways of Encountering the Same Authors   173

Index   175

GREAT MINDS

INTRODUCTION

In this book, we intend to introduce the reader to some authors who have made particularly significant, distinctive, and controversial contributions to the development of modern social theory. The latter is a body of scientifically oriented (and thus, as far as possible, empirically grounded) observations and interpretations regarding both social experience in general and the particular contents and forms it took with the emergence of modern culture and society. The authors in question were active between the middle of the 19th century and the second half of the following one. We have chosen to discuss only a relatively small number of these theorists, treating each in his own chapter, without systematically relating each to the others, and without explicitly comparing and contrasting positions with those taken by others.

This is of course a highly conventional arrangement of our materials. But we would like to characterize our treatment as *interpretive*, for throughout we:

Are highly selective

Consider only some of the themes each author has dealt with

Emphasize only what we consider the salient aspects of his thinking

Link, as far as possible, their work to a central vision that, we suggest, is exclusive to each author

In particular, each chapter seeks to identify in the first instance what we have called a given author's "philosophical anthropology," that is, his image of the human being, his understanding of the distinctive potentialities and vulnerabilities that orient, sustain, and constrain human individuals in constructing and managing their relations with one another. We start by considering these significant and original concerns as something of a common thread traceable throughout the majority of each author's writings, diverse as they may be.

This interpretive focus entails not seeking to summarize and evaluate each author's writings as a whole, reviewing them systematically and tracking their sources, or pointing to the large body of comments and criticisms of those writings by other authors. Rather, we aim to characterize *our* authors' views on issues still open in social theory discourse, for such views, we feel, continue to inspire, more or less explicitly and self-consciously, the positions taken on those issues in much contemporary sociological writing.

Why seek to introduce readers, as we suggest, to modern social theory by focusing on single authors from the remote or proximate past, rather than, say, on particular concepts, distinctive methodological approaches, or specific empirical inquiries? According to some critics, the insistence with which sociological debates refer back to the so-called classics, or to other significant writers whose major writings have appeared *at least* several decades ago, is a marker, or even a cause, of the scientific immaturity of the discipline. It suggests—allegedly—intellectual insecurity, unwillingness, or inability to advance by means of self-standing research undertakings, building on and thereby surpassing past contributions, or referring to them at most occasionally and perfunctorily. In contrast, they argue, mature sciences, beginning with the natural sciences, forget their founders, or at any rate do not consider revisiting their writings (much less holding a reverential attitude toward them) a necessary and significant component of their own intellectual mission. They work, one says, "cumulatively"; that is, each research undertaking builds only on the valid findings of immediately preceding ones, assuming that these have in turn assimilated and codified the valid findings of previous ones, and subjecting its own to the same process of selective acceptance or refusal by successive researchers. Even some social disciplines approach this model. Contemporary economists, for instance, do not consider themselves duty bound to read Adam Smith closely (if at all).

Now, undoubtedly and fortunately, also within sociology many contemporary research undertakings stand in such a "cumulative" relationship to preceding work. If, for instance, one compares research on social mobility from the 1950s with that from the last decade, one cannot help but see an irreversible progress that consigns many former inquiries to the forgettable past. The same can be said about the sociological literature addressing other research themes, from electoral behavior to family structures, from migration to deviance and criminality.

In spite of this, we find it wholly appropriate for contemporary sociological discourse to maintain a close relationship to a small number of authors more or less remote in time; engage in a self-conscious dialogue with their thinking;

and consider some of their writings a fundamental component in the intellectual formation of new generations of students, scholars, and researchers. We do so for two main reasons.

First, sociological discourse has a *non*cumulative dimension, which commits it to reflect at least occasionally on its own premises, its own intellectual and moral justifications. On this account, it refers back to previous confrontations with these themes, which over time have established themselves as most significant. Second, what we refer to as revisiting authors having, let us say, *canonical* status—assuming these authors are appropriately selected—affords contemporary readers, and particularly those just beginning to orient themselves within the sociological discipline, a unique opportunity to familiarize themselves with the legacies of extraordinary minds important or even foundational to the discipline. Readers can thus engage with writings that provide inspiring exemplars and models and that may shape and orient their own sociological imagination.

Such writings, furthermore, point out the futility of any kind of sociological sectarianism, the insistence of some contemporary sociologists on the necessity of placing rigid boundaries around what constitutes properly and exclusively sociological discourse. Contrarily, among the authors whom we treat, even those expressly committed to founding and promoting the discipline of sociology, giving it a distinctive substantial content and methodological profile, never hesitated to transgress its boundaries—by engaging in historical, philosophical, psychological, and economic discourse—when necessary to address problems more satisfactorily.

On the other hand, as already suggested, we are not seeking here to produce a concise "life and works" statement about our authors, undertake a close and sophisticated exegesis of individual writings, or identify once and for all "what is alive and what is dead" in their intellectual legacies. In fact, we believe that in contemporary sociological literature there is if anything an excess of such exegetical exercises and a tendency to consider all of an author's writing relevant. Moreover, we feel, in the writings of our authors the student often finds untenable or futile arguments, which may lead her into an intellectual blind alley. Thus we emphasize discussing those writings and those theoretical suggestions, insights, and problems we view as still *valuable* (which does not always mean *valid*). On this account they still deserve, so to speak, to be put in the spotlight to stimulate and evoke further reflection.

To the extent that we succeed in this task, we hope to lead readers to the further, potentially more fulfilling task of directly engaging the writings of these authors. (Acceptable translations of those not originally written in English are widely available, sometimes also online.)

Why did we choose *these* nine authors rather than others, or a greater number? The first four—Marx, Durkheim, Weber, and Simmel—have long been acknowledged as rightful members of the canon of modern social theory. We associate ourselves with this preference, and also (somewhat regretfully) with the current exclusion from the same canon of Vilfredo Pareto, an Italian author who for a time was reputed to deserve inclusion. We take equally for granted that, among contemporary authors, Talcott Parsons undoubtedly deserves to be considered. We think George Herbert Mead qualifies for a similar position; his ideas, after a period of neglect, have lately attracted much attention on the part of both sociologists and other social scientists. We would expect more objections to our choice of the remaining three authors—Garfinkel, Goffman, and Luhmann—and (perhaps even more) to our exclusion of such contemporaries of theirs as Foucault, Habermas, and Bourdieu. Garfinkel and Goffman, however, seem to us to have had (and to be having) a more significant impact on contemporary sociological work. They also enjoy a surplus of visibility and authoritativeness from having written and published while working in one or more great American universities. Goffman's writings, furthermore, have an advantage accruing from their remarkable literary qualities (a distinction alas not always shared by the other authors). A different reason led us to include Luhmann, with a chapter written specifically for this English edition: we consider him one of the major figures of European social thought, one who has received so far, in the English-speaking world, less critical attention than is deserved.

As we have already suggested, our greatest hope for this book is that it will induce readers to venture personally into the writings of one or more of the authors. To this end, we seek to offer enough information to enable readers to orient themselves in establishing direct contact with those primary sources. As a result, each chapter opens with a paragraph offering a brief biographical sketch of the author in question, including a brief list of what *we* consider his most significant works. The selection is unavoidably arbitrary and might easily be complemented by other titles, which for some reason *we* have not found equally informative and substantial. In drafting our chapters, however, we have made no reference to the life course of the authors, nor tried to locate them within the broader story of modern social theory, and have not referred to the large body of secondary literature dealing with them. This decision does not, of course, imply we do not acknowledge the validity of other scholarly approaches to our authors, or more broadly to sociological theory. To signal this, we close our book with a section that recommends a few valuable works in English to readers wishing to learn more about the "great minds" we discuss.

ACKNOWLEDGMENTS

The design of this book is the result of sustained conversation between the two authors. We have read all the chapters jointly many times and revised on the basis of our debates. We may, however, state that Gianfranco Poggi is responsible for the first four chapters and Giuseppe Sciortino for the last five.

When writing a book, of course, authors are never alone. We thank all those who have read and commented on earlier drafts of the chapters and of the book as a whole: Marzio Barbagli, Ivano Bison, Matteo Bortolini, Giancarlo Corsi, Martina Cvajner, Adam Haliburton, Nadya Jaworsky, Debora Mantovani, Licia Mignardi, Alberto Santambrogio, Stefani Scherer, Marcella Veglio. We are also grateful to the undergraduate and graduate students who have followed our classes on social theory ("classical" and contemporary) at Trento. Both of us have on several occasions adopted early drafts of various chapters as readings for classes taught in the United States and Canada. We are indebted to such "guinea pigs" for the comments they offered and for their inputs into our writing process.

1 KARL MARX

German philosopher and economist (1818–1883). He spent the greater part of his life in political exile, first in France then for many more years in England. Very active as an ideologist and leader of the working class movement within the International Working-men's Association (better known as the First International), he was involved, often with Friedrich Engels, in studies encompassing a broad selection of issues. A main theme of his writings is the criticism of how "political economists" treated major social affairs. Over against these, Marx and Engels sought to produce a scientific platform for the revolutionary fight of the working class against the bourgeois order. Marx's own writings received particular attention, and in many countries they came to constitute a theoretical charter for a number of significant trade unions and political parties, which on this account are often characterized as "Marxist"—a term also referring to the various thinkers inspired by and sympathetic to his work. One of these parties, led by Lenin, was the winning protagonist of the Russian revolution of October 1917, and since its fateful success the term *Marxist* has also been applied to several movements and to the political regimes of various countries.

SUGGESTED READINGS
Economic and Philosophical Manuscript of 1844, and *The Communist Manifesto*,
    Prometheus Books, Amherst, New York, 1988.
The German Ideology Including Theses on Feuerbach, Prometheus, 1998.
Capital: A Critique of Political Economy, Penguin, London, 1992.

A S IS THE CASE with other social theorists, all of Marx's thought unfolds against the background of a more or less explicit understanding of the nature of human beings—what renders them different from other forms of animal life and determines, more or less directly, how they organize and manage their social existence. Aristotle, for instance, characterizes the human being as a "political animal"; Adam Smith views the propensity of individuals to undertake exchanges with one another as central to human nature. Marx, in turn, largely subscribes to a conception of the human being often conveyed by the Latin expression *homo faber*, literally "man the smith" but more often translated as "man the maker."

In this conception, human beings are distinguished from other animals by their being compelled, and enabled, to provide for their own subsistence by means of a peculiar form of activity we may call *production*. In this activity, which for human beings (as for all other animals) responds in the first place to the need to maintain the existence of the single being, allowing it to reproduce itself, humans also deal with the natural world, but in doing so they avail themselves of objects not made available to them by nature itself but brought into being by humans themselves in order to control nature, defend themselves from it, and place its resources at the service of their wants and desires.

Humans can manipulate and modify the materials of nature by adding their own activity or labor, thereby turning these elements into new instruments of future activity. The capacity of the species for certain mental activities enables humans to follow this course. They can examine the extant circumstances, form judgments and preferences that inspire their efforts to bring about imagined conditions, and endeavor to realize those conditions. By this account, such operations differ from one human group to another, and from one phase to another in each group's experience. In this sense, the human species is endowed with creativity, in that its activity can modify the circumstances of its own existence and thus to some extent express, develop, and realize diverse potentialities.

Marx is indebted for these ideas to the idealistic tradition in German philosophy, and to the Romantic sensitivity, well established in his own generation. But he differs from his predecessors, who emphasized only the loftiest and noblest human creations (institutions expressing the community's values, myths, beliefs, understandings of reality, aesthetic experiences). Marx insistently stresses, by contrast, that human creativity is chiefly the ability to intervene upon nature, and upon the legacy of earlier interventions, to produce resources that allow men to nourish themselves, protect themselves from environmental threats, and permit the burgeoning of new generations. But within the various contexts thus emerging, all originating from the experience of *need*, emerge also the contradictions of human social life, which in turn determine the dynamics of history. Marx emphasizes:

> The fundamental part played in human existence by processes related to the production of material life, a part long ignored or belittled in particular by philosophers

The role performed within those processes by the "means of production," which at any given time constitute a bridge, as it were, between past and present productive activity

The possibility that the means of production come under the privileged control of other subjects than those directly engaged in production, owing to certain institutions, the most significant of which is private property

The essentially (though not always overtly) antagonistic nature of the relationship between those who appropriate the means of production and those who put them to use in their own productive activity under conditions dictated by their inferior status vis-à-vis the appropriators

Thus, according to Marx all historic societies are more or less overtly fissured by a fundamental division related to the processes of production and distribution of resources, shaped by the technological equipment every society develops and deploys to control and exploit nature. But such equipment, in turn, can be brought into being and employed only by means of *social* relations, that is relations between individuals, or rather between the collectivities those individuals make up. Marx calls the most significant such collectivities "classes." They develop and operate in the context of production and distribution, and for this reason they stand in a basically antagonistic relationship to one another.

Why so? When all is said and done, *one* class consumes more than it produces because *the other* produces more than it consumes. The first maintains an advantageous position by controlling the means of production, allowing itself to establish and maintain an exploitative relationship with the other class. Consequently, every society is characterized by social inequality, by the asymmetry between the classes concerning the direct involvement of the respective members in the production process, and by those members' access to both the resources employed in that process and the goods and services it yields. Hence the fundamental conflict between the interest of one class in maintaining and increasing such inequalities and the other's interest in moderating or suppressing them.

In Marx's thought, however, the processes revolving around the functioning and maintenance of a given society are also those that in the long run account for the changes occurring in it. The very inequalities that in a given society allow a minority to control and exploit the majority's productive activities at the same time put the society under pressure. They induce the majority to *seek* to subvert a relationship that prevents its access to and enjoyment of the very wealth it has labored to produce.

We emphasize *seek* because this second aspect of the structured inequality rarely manifests itself in an actual, dramatic subversion of existent social reality. More often, the majority's resistance is covert and silent, and its interests remain systematically subordinate to those of the minority, in spite of the antagonism between the former and the latter. Usually, indeed, the majority is not even conscious of its distinctive interests and of its contrast with those of the exploitative class, or at any rate the majority does not explicitly and effectively pursue its own interests. Why should this be the case?

CONTROL OVER THE MEANS OF PRODUCTION

One can impute this phenomenon, in generic terms, to a principle asserted by Marx against the idealistic tradition: the processes of human existence wherein material life is produced have an intrinsic priority with respect to all other processes. Very crudely: whoever controls production and distribution of the wealth of societies controls everything in society, as far as it can be controlled.

This does not deny all significance to other aspects of social experience—religion, art, kinship relations, and law. Nonetheless, exactly because of their significance, these components cannot but be seriously shaped and biased, and to an extent determined, by the way in which, in a given society, production and distribution of wealth are organized and managed. All other aspects can only, more or less explicitly and directly, respect and as far as possible promote the interests of the class possessing itself of the means of production, and by the same token oppose those of the dispossessed and exploited class, or at any rate allow that class to pursue its own interests only if and to the extent that they remain compatible with the society's current structure.

Take *religion*, for instance. According to Marx, all religion expresses some dissatisfaction and unease toward existence as experienced by the believer. It articulates a yearning for a world more coherent and just than the existent one, an aspiration toward values belittled and denied by mundane, daily experience. However, religion basically "transmogrifies" these yearnings by addressing them to an imaginary world beyond. It leads the believer first to adopt a suffering but resigned attitude, and second not to seek to realize those aspirations in the here and now, which would require subverting the productive relations of society.

These relations, in fact, induce the believer to form those yearnings and give them some expression (in prayer, for instance), but at the same time frustrate them. In this way, consciously or unconsciously, for its adherents religion becomes an accomplice of the existent state of affairs, even when it evokes values (justice, freedom, brotherhood) that the state of affairs prevents the great majority of human beings from experiencing and enjoying.

In the same manner, a society's *law* constitutes for all individuals a point of reference, a set of public, sanctioned expectations to which they refer in orienting and managing their existence, controlling its uncertainties and risks. In every society, though, the legal arrangements reflect and uphold the priority of the interests of the dominant class over against those of the dominated class. The measure of security and predictability they confer on the latter's existence does not contradict the subordinate position of the dominated class; rather, it secures its subordination.

Consider, finally, *political power*. As Marx sees the matter, all its forms share the function of placing at the service of a society's decisional center an ensemble of material, organizational, and symbolic resources it may employ to institute and sanction (if necessary by force) a binding order of social relations, to deploy or threaten organized violence against those who violate or challenge that order. But this order, as we have seen, is centered on the dominant class's control over the productive forces and the related arrangements for producing and distributing wealth. Therefore, political power itself, even when concentrated into expressly political institutions separated from those directly related to material production, and when it claims to be the guardian of the interests of society as a whole (as is the case with the modern state), necessarily sanctions and justifies the interests of the society's ruling class.

One might extend this argument to the aesthetic preferences and practices prevalent in a society, the forms of knowledge it harbors and produces, the institutions concerned with sexual expression, the family, education—in fact, to all social processes *not* directly pertaining to producing and distributing a society's material resources. In some texts, to synthesize this position Marx distinguishes between a society's economic base and an ideological superstructure. The several components (legal, political, aesthetic, religious, intellectual, etc.) of the latter may expressly affirm the intrinsic superiority of the class controlling material resources and mandate subordination of the class excluded from them.

Alternatively, they may make the latter's position less burdensome, allowing its components to manage their existence with a degree of security and gratification, and orient that existence to beliefs, norms, and values that to some extent endow it with meaning.

If this is so, how can one account for the fact that history presents episodes of radical change, when existing arrangements are forcefully subverted and the rule of one class over all of society is more or less rapidly and radically suppressed? Marx's answer to this query refers again to *homo faber*, to the inherent creativity of the human species, its capacity to contrive ever new ways of controlling and mastering nature. The most easily perceived expressions of this capacity concern material technology; consider the transition from the water mill to the steam mill, or to the invention of stirrups as a riding implement. But typically the adoption and diffusion of such innovations require new relations between those employing them, for instance new ways of selecting, training, and disciplining those immediately involved in their productive use; of dividing and coordinating their activities; and so on.

Marx views every new technique and the associated system of relations as a wider and more mature expression of human creativity, which adds to the wealth available to society. As such, new techniques and new relations threaten, we would say today, the "sustainability" of the existent patterns of production and distribution. They entitle new minorities to gain mastery of production processes, and render obsolete present-day institutions and cultural forms, since these are (as we have seen) components of the social condition that such innovations would overturn. These developments, then, threaten social hierarchies, eroding the effectiveness and legitimacy of the current ruling class in managing the social process as a whole. Confronted with such a challenge, this class at first seeks stubbornly to reaffirm its privileges. It contrasts the development and diffusion of the new productive forces and relations, and it denies the legitimacy of new leading groups. Its resistance to change may be successful over a shorter or longer period, sometimes by deploying political violence to beat back and suppress the developments threatening it, sometimes by appealing to long-established values and habits that have not lost their hold on the minds of people and that attach people to some extent to the present conditions, or at any rate leave them resigned to the persistence of those conditions.

However, a massive, drastic turn in the historical process is possible under three conditions. First, the contrast between the current situation and the new potentialities opened by productive innovations must become glaring. Second, the groups responsible for such innovations and capable of managing them must effectively challenge and overpower their opponents and compel them to accept the change. Finally, every major turn requires, more or less directly, the development of new institutional arrangements and cultural resources, capable of displacing those still present in fields as diverse as (again) religion, law, political arrangements, artistic expression, and kinship relations.

On this account, fundamental turns in historical development are necessarily few and far between and typically, according to Marx, take place through social revolutions. They correspond with epochal changes in the relationship between the human species and the rest of nature, liberate unprecedented productive forces, and require formation of new groups capable of enacting these changes and successfully establishing themselves as the new ruling class.

Such groups have always envisaged, and have been chiefly inspired by, their own particular interests, and have always brought into being new forms of social division and exploitation. In spite of that, Marx thinks, such changes, however unintentionally, display new and broader potentialities of the species, affirm more general interests, reveal needs and capacities of the human being as such, and transcend the bonds and constraints of the previous condition. For this reason, to constitute progress every massive change must treat the current situation as its own premise, deny its validity and legitimacy, suppress it, but at the same time realize its implicit promise.

Between these rare and intense moments of change, history does not stand still. Minor, marginal innovations often take place, and the dominated class may variously resist exploitation without suppressing it (or indeed may see its own condition worsen). Finally, law, art, science, and religion may see changes in their content and form. Political units, in particular, may be ruled by successive sovereigns or dynasties, wage war, acquire or lose territory, and modify their own military, judicial, and fiscal arrangements. Populations may wax or wane. Their social composition may become more varied and complex than suggested by the simple contrast of ruling class and ruled-over class; such variety may manifest itself in diverse and changing alignments of groups, in significant changes in the ways individuals define their own identity and their own interests, or how they form groupings that in turn relate to one another.

Marx is aware of these diverse manifestations of the historical nature of human events, and he acknowledges their significance. But he insists on the prior import of innovations related to productive structures and processes and on the extent to which their impact turns history into a coherent whole, marked by progress—though a progress pushed forward by antagonism, by one class forcefully asserting its interests over those of others.

Historical experience as a whole, once beyond its most primitive phase— where human populations behaved not so differently from nonhuman ones— can be summarized as a succession of three "modes of production." Each is characterized by how the surplus production made possible by technology and the associated division of labor is manipulated and placed under the control of the nonproducing minority.

The *ancient* mode of production is characterized by enslavement of the productive majority. Its members are owned by other people, who buy and sell them as mere material tools and control completely the form and product of their activities. In the *feudal* mode, the producers (typically, the serfs) are politically dependent on and subordinate to nonproducers, lords who compel them to perform unpaid labor and deliver to them part of the product of the labor the serfs perform in relative autonomy. In the *capitalist/bourgeois* mode, the relations between producers and nonproducers present themselves as con-tractual in nature; that is, the former sell the latter their own labor power at the current market rate. However, workers do so in a condition of objective inferiority, because they lack control over the means of production. Thus the capitalists/bourgeois (who own those means) basically dictate the terms of employment. In this way, they establish and manage a historically novel form of exploitation, less glaringly unequal than the previous ones, and particularly dynamic because it yields profits through market exchanges under competi-tive conditions.

This elementary narrative of the whole history of humanity is starkly (indeed brutally) simple, and it may be justified only as one component of an histori-cal overview (at most) of the advance of the West toward modernity. In fact, in one text where he presents this narrative, Marx complements it with a brief, cryptic reference to an *Asiatic* mode of production—little more than a glimpse of the *remainder* of historical experience. (Some glimpses at prehistorical ex-perience, and at the conditions of the few remaining "primitive" populations, can be found in "Forms Which Precede the Capitalist Mode of Production," part of a long manuscript left unpublished by Marx and generally referred to as *The Grundrisse*.

ANALYSIS OF THE CAPITALIST MODE OF PRODUCTION

Marx's social theory basically aims to describe and explain the distinctive, historically unique traits of the modern condition produced in Europe by the advent of capitalism, particularly in its more recent, industrial phase, which Marx was able to observe and criticize from close up in England. His whole protracted, complex, original scholarly work was intended as the intellectual instrument of the socialist revolution. This would defeat the capitalist system, and establish for the first time in human experience a society not fissured by division and driven by conflict, not developing through the clash of partial, antagonistic interests among its parts. Here the control of the human species over the rest of nature would at last be fully displayed, and the unfolding of its productive potential would cease to be powered by exploitation. Only at this point, Marx wrote, would the *pre*history of humankind cease and its *history* proper begin.

Consequently, the greater part of Marx's gigantic intellectual effort (mostly motivated by his own aspiration to lead, or at any rate to orient theoretically, the struggle of the working class against capitalist society) was focused on the specifically capitalistic form of the production and distribution of material wealth. This effort mainly took the form of a "critique of political economy," the understanding of capitalism that Marx's contemporaries proposed and underwrote.

In that understanding, as we have already suggested, the employment relation at the center of the capitalist mode of production constitutes a proper contractual exchange of labor power for salary; it is a voluntarily and expressly entered legal relation between two equals, the worker and the capitalist. Marx argues however that this construction of it is superficial and fallacious, concealing the true nature of the relation. This, in his view, entails a subjection of the worker (or proletarian, as Marx often puts it) to the capitalist, comparable to (though different from) that between the ancient slave and the master, or the medieval serf and the feudal lord. What all such relations involve is, at bottom, exploitation.

Marx labored to present this complex and demanding argument so many times, so diffusely, in so many ways—sometimes in writings left unfinished and unpublished—that one may suspect he himself harbored doubts about its ultimate scientific tenability. In any case, it is not necessary here to expound Marx's argument because it belongs, in substance, to the history of economic rather than sociological thought. Furthermore, it is mostly carried out starting from philosophical premises and in a mode of analysis belonging to a phase in the development of economic thought long left behind. Finally, there are reasons for thinking that in the end this argument, however forcefully and imaginatively put forward, is not intrinsically valid and compelling. In what follows, though we have suggested that the capitalist mode of production belongs to the essence of modern society (or indeed determines it), we seek to summarize Marx's more properly sociological conception of modern society, rather than his view and critique of its mode of production.

To begin with, the historical peculiarity of modern society reveals itself in the character of the two classes that are the chief collective actors or protagonists of its existence: the bourgeoisie and the working class. The former is composed of individuals directly involved in productive activities, though not as immediate producers but as the owners of capital. The property they own and manage, unlike the patrimony of premodern property-owning classes, comprises an ensemble of productive resources requiring activities that engage the owners themselves— activities aimed at producing profit through market transactions: "The wealth of those societies in which the capitalist mode of production prevails presents itself as 'an immense collection of commodities'" (Marx, 2000: 458).

Commodities constitute not only the objects the system produces for the market but also those gathered, organized, and managed by capitalists in order to commit them to such production. Furthermore, labor power, which carries out productive activity, is itself a commodity. On this account, the whole system presupposes the existence of money, and its dynamic rests on a particular configuration of the relationship between commodity (C) and money (M). In some systems, M intervenes solely to mediate the relation between a commodity C_1 that a subject has and a commodity C_2 that it does not have but acquires by selling C_1. In the capitalist process, however, we see a sum of money M_1 that is expended to acquire a commodity C in the intent of attaining in the end a sum M_2. But since, unlike commodities, money does not present qualitative differences (such as those motivating the sequence $C_1 - C_2$), this $M_1 - C - M_2$ sequence makes sense only if M_2 is in fact M+; that is to say, the sum of money at the end of the sequence is greater than at the beginning.

By the same token, the M1 − C − M+ sequence tends to repeat itself, to represent a single moment in a potentially infinite progression (which does not hold for C1 − M − C2). This observation already captures the dynamic characteristic of the capitalist system: its tendency to generate continuous movement. It also suggests a question: What kind of commodity allows the repeated passage from a given sum of money to a greater sum (M1 − C − M+)?

According to Marx, the commodity in question can only be labor power, acquired by the employer on the market and expended by the worker under the employer's control. The arguments to this effect (advanced by Marx many times in varying forms) are part of the economic discourse we prefer not to consider here. Sociologically, though, one can ask under what conditions the capitalist owners of M may in fact find on the market a labor force and commit it to the productive process under its own control, operating with means of production themselves acquired on the market. The answer is simple: this is possible if and only insofar as the owners of labor power themselves are *exclusively* owners of labor power, given that the productive resources of significance within the economic system are all firmly under the control of the capitalists, in the form of money or (above all) as *organized* ensembles of forces of production—most typically, those represented by industrial factories.

This situation, in turn, is the result of a process of accumulation of resources where innovation plays a central role by developing material and organizational technologies that drastically diminish the import, and the strategic relevance for the society as a whole, of traditional forms of wealth and sources of sustenance. In particular, the context of the rise of capitalism is characterized by the growing significance of monetary resources invested in commercial and manufacturing rather than agricultural activities, or in new, market-oriented, commercialized ways of managing landed estates. That context further entails the suppression of ancient, communal use of resources on the part of villagers who, once thus deprived of a significant part of their traditional means of subsistence, are compelled to sell their labor power.

Furthermore, the capitalist owners of the new productive resources, because they sell on the market the commodities thus produced, are led by the pressure of competition to constantly add to and modify those resources. In particular, this accounts for the progressive replacement of the traditional tools and practices of craftsmen by machine-assisted production; the shift of this from the workers' own households to larger and larger industrial sites; the growing significance, among the products, of objects destined to further production over those intended for immediate consumption; and the new modalities of distribution of products (from the village fair to larger, twenty-four-hour stores; from the local scope of the market to its national, and finally to its global scope). Basically, the new, capitalistic mode of production is associated with new modalities of the man-nature relationship, which find their most visible expression in larger and larger industrial factories whose product is destined for increasing numbers of distant, changing, anonymous buyers.

These phenomena display the dynamic tendencies of the $M - C - M+$ cycle, its nature as a process of "creative destruction." Goaded by competition and aimed at profit, the process unceasingly challenges established forms of production and the modalities of labor power expenditure and consumption, and at the same time it establishes others. It is associated with a huge increase in and diversification of society's wealth, in the possibilities of enjoyment and experience open to individuals. The process entails massive changes in numerous aspects of how individuals relate to one another, in how they conceive of themselves and of the surrounding reality.

Traditionally privileged social groups, such as the aristocracy or urban corporations whose economic activities involved traditional techniques and practices, find themselves surpassed and displaced by the protagonists of industrial production and lose their advantageous position in the social hierarchy. Increasingly rapid urbanization deprives the countryside of growing segments of its population. The countryside itself, previously the site of the dominant kind of economic activity, becomes the site of superannuated practices, values, and beliefs; it witnesses, in the larger social context, the loss of prestige and credibility suffered by tradition. New forms of knowledge become central to the society's culture, produced chiefly in cities and grounded in expanding literacy, the diffusion of printing, and the emergence of new, specialized institutions for education and research. All this in turn generates new, secular ways of apprehending and comprehending reality, of programming and assessing forms of social conduct, which challenge the standing of religious knowledge and the prestige of ecclesiastical hierarchies.

Further changes affect the structures for formation of public policy and its administrative implementation. Political processes open themselves to the representation and participation of broader sections of the population, reflect and amplify the values and interests of new leading social groups, register the orientation of currents of public opinion, produce new rules for collective existence, and cope (well or otherwise) with an ever more complex and changing social reality in which unprecedented needs and opportunities ceaselessly emerge.

Finally, Western societies interact with one another more openly, due to the broadening of markets and the unceasing and expanding traffic in goods, capital, knowledge, and individuals. These interactions increasingly affect the rest of the world, both through formation of colonial empires and by conveying the irresistible impact of industrial progress. The face of the earth is slowly modified by new ways of communication and forms of transport, shifting the boundaries between some political units and allowing others to attain a continental scope and engage in colonial ventures. This process progressively conveys to the world as a whole the models and values of modern Western culture, rendering them ever more secular, individualistic, and materialistic.

Marx considers all these developments a distinctive, valuable achievement of the new, bourgeois ruling class, because they develop and assert ever broader, more diverse, and more authentic human potentialities. But even though in this way the bourgeoisie liberates immense productive powers, from which the whole society—indeed humankind itself—can benefit, it does so only in the relentless pursuit of its own class interests. For this reason, bourgeois achievement can make only a limited and sometimes contradictory contribution to an authentic emancipation that would effectively benefit the whole of society, and indeed, through the inevitable expansion of modern, Western technology and culture, the whole human species.

For example, the constitutional developments taking place in the West afford its citizens opportunities for political participation and mobilization; but these opportunities do not seriously impinge on economic inequality and the position of inferiority it generates for the majority of the population.

Legal systems become more complex and sophisticated and appeal to procedures of a rational nature, but they assert and proclaim the centrality of institutions—private property, contracts, the firm, the market—through which societies remain divided into unequal parts with conflicting interests.

Modern culture increasingly emphasizes science and thus bodies of verifiable and practicable knowledge; it frees the collective mentality from the misapprehensions and delusions characteristic of religious thinking. At the same time, it often replaces them with new misunderstandings and delusions, focused on the state, the nation, money, and the market. The increasingly dominant mentality is often petty, egoistic, and greedy, and it leaves less room for sentiments of solidarity and generosity, for disinterested attitudes, and for aesthetic sensitivity. Family life revolves increasingly around economic priorities, which marginalize other concerns and emotions. The typical individual of modern society is a tense being, ceaselessly tormented by the pressure of need and the aspiration to new gains.

Although for Marx modern bourgeois society constitutes undeniable progress over previous historical societies, it has many aspects that justify strong criticism or even outright condemnation. This is due, essentially, to the production system on which this society is grounded, which according to Marx, as we have seen, entails a form of exploitation that, although representing a great historical advance, nevertheless remains inexorable and basically immoral. Every moment of a worker's time at work is exchanged for a part of the salary he has contracted with the employer, but in fact the worker is allowed to work for his own subsistence, and thus is allowed to live, only if for a certain portion of his working time his work for the capitalist remains unpaid. Within capitalism, alienation takes place to the extent that workers are made to work more hours than are incorporated into the goods they consume.

As was already suggested, there are reasons for doubting the validity of arguments Marx puts forward, to the effect that the capitalist mode of production necessarily entails exploitation. Again, we are solely interested in the sociological component of those arguments, particularly as they suggest that its very dynamic leads capitalism to its own demise. In all the countries where this mode of production and bourgeois rule are established or advancing, the working class struggles to organize, improve its own situation, and contrast the bourgeoisie's hold on society as a whole; at times, it seeks through union or political activities to subvert the entire social order.

Motivated by his own profound hostility toward the social and political arrangements the bourgeoisie imposes, and by his commitment to the project of their suppression, Marx engaged in political activities as a publicist and as a contender for leadership in contemporary workers' organizations. At the same time, his scholarly writings align themselves strongly with workers' struggles, seek to orient them theoretically, argue the reasons for them, and suggest their strategy.

There are two main phases to this protracted intellectual engagement. The first is represented chiefly by the writings of "the young Marx," especially those produced during his stay in Paris in the 1840s. Here, on the one hand, Marx confronted for the first time the political economy literature from Britain, which opened up for him an intellectual horizon previously ignored when he was dealing chiefly with philosophical questions (albeit already in a radical mode). On the other hand, for the first time he came across the associational activities of factory workers, deriving from such experience a sense for what might be called the subjective dimension of the worker's condition under the capitalist regime.

Accordingly, his writings of this phase (the most significant of them not intended for publication) address the typical life conditions of contemporary industrial workers, compelled, in order to gain a salary, to place their own labor power at the disposal of employers who engage it in work with industrial machines within factories. To characterize this specific (and increasingly significant) condition, Marx chiefly uses the expression "alienation," taking it from Hegelian philosophical language.

What is suggested by this? The human capacity to produce and create manifests quite openly in the unending and ever-changing stream of objects the capitalist produces. However, the workers experience in a particularly acute manner the dispossession of their own forces and their lack of any control over their own products. Concretely, the worker feels alienated from the objects he produces, from his own working activity, from himself, and from the other individuals he collaborates with. Marx seeks the reasons for this multiple experience of alienation. He argues that the suffering it inflicts on the worker must be due to the enjoyment it provides for others; that the worker feels dispossessed because someone else is appropriating his labor and benefits from doing so.

In a second, much longer phase, Marx undertakes an insightful, imaginative, and elaborate reconstruction of the formation of the working class, as a counterpart to that of the bourgeoisie. However, he pays relatively little attention to the latter, for he views the bourgeoisie as nothing else than the carrier of the interests of capital, who in this capacity accumulates, modifies, and manages collective resources ultimately generated by others. It is these others who attract Marx's attention, on various accounts. First there is the moral solidarity that the workers' sufferings continue to evoke in him. Then "Marx the economist" holds that throughout history it is the direct producers—the exploited, consuming much less than they produce—who through their efforts bear the burden of the entire process of wealth production, by generating "value." Finally, for this very reason they can realize *their* interests only by propelling society toward the socialist revolution, with which the history of humanity will finally begin.

Marx focuses on England for his account of the complex and prolonged events leading to formation of the working class. They begin with the so-called enclosures, which partitioned land into privately owned portions to be bought and sold, denying the rural population access to communal resources that traditionally allowed households to support their own existence. Consequently, Marx describes the forcible expulsion from the land of a significant part of that population, condemning it to seek subsistence from employment in the nascent industrial system, and above all in the factory sector, where the emergent working class is subjected to oppressive and humiliating conditions that Marx documents and criticizes.

In this context, the young Marx's original, philosophically inspired reflections on alienation yield (especially in *Capital*) to an empirically grounded discourse. He describes, in particular, how the labor of women and children was savagely used and abused by employers; the factory's systematic recourse to increasingly efficient and profitable machinery demanding more continuous and intense effort on the part of workers; the effect of these practices on their condition; and the resistance by employers to any attempt to limit the duration of the working day. Marx was certainly not the first to notice and discuss these phenomena. When young, his lifelong associate Engels had already analyzed some of them, and numerous other observers and critics had long since revealed these and other aspects of "the social question" from diverse viewpoints. But Marx's scholarly confrontation with these issues was unequaled in width and depth, and in its political resonance.

Furthermore, Marx's retrospective arguments set the background for a penetrating sociological analysis, originally foreshadowed in *The Communist Manifesto* (1848). He does not simply register and condemn the situation of the ever-growing industrial proletariat but observes and justifies its resistance to that situation. He proposes and seeks to advance conscious, resolute, effective forms of class struggle, whereby a new collective subject, the working class (organized into unions and parties) may oppose the strategy of the bourgeoisie and promotes its own revolution. In this context, Marx masterfully examines why the advance of capitalism itself, against its own interests, makes such developments inevitable, and he unceasingly promotes his own view of how the proletariat should wage the class struggle. In writings that are not primarily scholarly in nature, he seeks to commit to this view the international workers' movement and criticizes, in an often overly aggressive, sectarian, and intolerant manner, the alternative views put forward by other leaders.

Here we are concerned solely with the first line of discourse. Marx holds that in seeking to accumulate capital by its unceasing search for profits, the bourgeoisie unavoidably gathers unprecedented numbers of workers (originally, those the enclosures had expelled from the countryside) into larger factories and larger urban centers. Uprooted from their original communities (villages, craft guilds), workers encounter new conditions allowing and indeed compelling them to become aware of one another, of the shared interests related to their new, punishing circumstances. Progressively acknowledging the contrast between such interests and those of the employers (generally upheld by the legal system, and by the government's political and administrative practices), workers seek to act on their own interests, organize themselves (in spite of the sacrifices this entails, and often experiencing defeat), and identify occasions and issues that would cause them to mobilize themselves in pursuit of collective objectives.

These processes are unintentionally promoted by further strategies of the capitalist class, which according to Marx render more visible and politically and morally less acceptable the divergence between the economic and social conditions of its own existence and that of the workers. By subjecting workers to closer and more despotic control over their productive activities, employers condemn them to increasing deprivation and risk, including that of unemployment.

THE UNSUSTAINABILITY OF CAPITALISM

A final theme in Marx's thinking on the capitalist condition is the view that it is intrinsically unsustainable; its very logic condemns it to self-abolition and makes the socialist revolution inevitable. He articulates this view, however, by means of two distinct arguments, not easily rendered compatible, each of which holds the center in different writings and assigns the other a subordinate position.

On the one hand, Marx emphasizes what we may call the *subjective* component of the revolutionary perspective, appealing to the considerations we have just recalled on the working class's growing maturity, awareness of shared interests, and capacity for organization and collective initiative. He expects the class struggle to shift its locus increasingly to the political level, and there, instead of seeking merely to ameliorate the immediate circumstances of the working class, to challenge the entire bourgeois ordering of society. Ultimately—he expects— the class's leading elements, constituted into a party, will expressly undertake total subversion of that order—a task that, as previous revolutions have shown, requires recourse to collective violence.

There is also what one may call an *objective* argument, where the internal contradictions of the capitalist system render it unable to fully develop productive forces and promote continuous growth of wealth. The basic contradiction is that the system evokes and commits all social resources, including those of science and technology, but it does so anarchically and often destructively, pushed as it is by antagonism between private interests leading to competition between firms. For this reason, capitalist development cannot be controlled by a conscious process of collective choice, oriented to the interest of the whole society.

This contradiction is manifested in various ways. In particular, the capitalist periodically suffers crises, when wealth is destroyed instead of produced, and there is a surplus of commodities over the purchasing power of the population, a growing part of which is condemned to unemployment. Competition between firms is, as we saw, the engine of the economic process, but it often limits and subverts itself through formation of fewer, larger firms, which aspire to become monopolies and thus bypass competition. Furthermore—and here the argument appeals to economic considerations that once more we leave aside, given both their complexity and the serious doubts concerning their tenability—the practices that are intended to increase the entity of the profits accumulated in the short run by individual firms tend in the medium and long run to reduce the *rate* of profit for the system as a whole.

Especially in his later writings, Marx insistently and pressingly advanced the thesis of the *Zusammenbruch* (total breakdown, collapse) that awaits the capitalist system in the more-or-less imminent future. He (unduly) considered this development inevitable, on objective grounds; but this *objective* view conflicted with the *subjective* one, focused on the theoretical and practical elaboration of effective strategies for class struggle. The fact is that both theses coexist in Marx's work, and he did not seem to perceive their contrast. However, that contrast was destined to manifest itself, sometimes with grave consequences, in the later history of workers' movements and parties that appealed to Marx's thinking for their own inspiration and orientation.

Finally, one may note that Marx paid little attention to a significant question: What kind of society would be brought into being by either the *Zusammenbruch* of the capitalist system or its suppression by the revolutionary workers' movement? In principle, this vital query could have been a fruitful subject for sociological reflection, but Marx did not want to follow other thinkers of the socialist tradition by engaging in utopian speculations over a future that he aspired to and considered unavoidable, but whose institutional make-up he considered it futile (or dangerous) to envision and describe. Certainly, he felt, in postrevolutionary society the fundamental relationship between humankind and the rest of nature—the ever-increasing, technologically assisted mastery of the former over the latter—would no longer be grounded in the struggle between opposing interests (those of the two basic classes or those of competing elements of the bourgeoisie) but instead would be collectively managed in a comprehensive, conscious manner. This would allow the unfolding of infinite human possibilities, placing them in the service of the entire collectivity and no longer primarily of one part of it.

This development would culminate in a situation that Marx barely sketches, proposing two rather different images of it in the first and last phases of his itinerary as a revolutionary thinker. In 1846, in their joint work (left unpublished) *The German Ideology*, Marx and Engels foresee a condition in which the division of labor has been abolished, in which

nobody has one exclusive sphere of activity but each can become accomplished in any branch he wishes, society regulates the general production and thus makes it possible for me to do one thing today and another tomorrow, to hunt in the morning, fish in the afternoon, rear cattle in the evening, criticize after dinner, just as I have a mind, without ever becoming hunter, fisherman, cowherd, or critic [Marx, 2000: 185].

In a much later piece of writing (1875), Marx characterizes the highest attainment of the forthcoming socialist revolution—communist society—by invoking the slogan "from each according to his ability, to each according to his needs!" (Marx, 2000: 615).

Leaving aside various (and serious) sociological objections to either image of the ultimate society, one may impute to Marx a culpable lack of reflection on *how* such a society was to manage the entire social process consciously and collectively, and in particular on the management role assigned to the state, to law, or to democratic institutions. Once more, this lack of reflection, lack of a sustained effort to project this society and not just fantasize about it, and the utter inadequacy of the few writings where Marx sought to remedy such deficit, was to have massive (and disastrous) practical consequences for the operations of various components of the international workers' movement, especially in the first part of the twentieth century. However, it is not this chapter's task to discuss those and other practical outcomes, direct or indirect, of Marx's own thought, but merely to present its most significant theoretical components.

REFERENCES
Marx, Karl, *Selected Writings*, Oxford University Press, Oxford, 2000.

2 EMILE DURKHEIM

French scholar of Jewish descent (1858–1917). After extended philosophical studies, he devoted his life, both as a scholar and as an academic leader, to establishing the discipline of sociology in the French university system. He affirmed the scientific autonomy of the discipline and defined its conceptual and methodological features with respect to other disciplines. Inspired by strong Republican sentiments, he expected sociology to contribute to the health of the Republic through programs of social reform aimed at what he considered the major structural weaknesses of contemporary society.

SUGGESTED READINGS
The Division of Labour in Society, Free Press, New York, 1997.
Rules of Sociological Method, Free Press, 1982.
On Suicide, Penguin, New York, 2007.
The Elementary Forms of Religious Life, Free Press, 1995.
Professional Ethics and Civil Morals, Routledge, London, 1992.
L'individualisme et les intellectuels, 1898, http://classiques.uqac.ca/classiques/Durkheim
    _emile/sc_soc_et_action/texte_3_10/individualisme.pdf

O NE CAN DETECT also in Durkheim's thought (as in Marx's) a *philosophical anthropology*, a view of those qualities that differentiate the human species from others, attribute to the species a peculiar relationship to nature, and underlie the tensions and dilemmas characterizing the human experience in its most diverse manifestations across time and space. According to Durkheim, what is most distinctive about mankind is the "dualism" of its very nature. (He expresses this also by speaking of *homo duplex*, twofold man.) What does this mean?

As with any other animal species, humans exist only as individuals; but two components operate in the mental life of each one of them. The first is directly grounded in the individual's bodily, sensorial apparatus and primarily concerns desires and activities related to the natural needs associated with its path from birth to death. The second component, however, is constituted by expectations, beliefs, aspirations, understandings, and values that primarily derive from and in turn orient each individual's relationship to others, and manifest themselves in activities expressing solidarity, indifference, or hostility toward some of them.

From Durkheim's writings, one can derive a few statements about the relationship between these two components:

The second component owes its existence to the fact that, more than any other animal, each human being is necessarily engaged in relationships with fellow human beings; thus it is the source of the vast majority of the contents of the individual's mind.

For the same reason, these contents are inevitably historical; that is, they vary over time and space.

These contents are not simply juxtaposed with the bodily and sensory human apparatus; it is their task—while registering the passions, instincts, and behavioral modalities that derive spontaneously from that apparatus—to assert their superiority over the first component, orienting the individual's sentiments and activities toward needs and preferences beyond its own immediate survival and physical well-being.

However, the superiority of the second component over the first, though justified and necessary, is intrinsically problematic. It does not result automatically from merely natural processes; nor does it spontaneously generate congruent behavioral tendencies. Instead, it manifests itself by shaping after its own image, so to speak, the tendencies arising from the first component, or where necessary by denying them expression and repressing them. At the same time, the first component is not docile. Rather, it contrasts and resists the disciplines the second seeks to impose on it.

Therefore the relationship between the two components is irreducibly contingent; it is never certain which in any specific case will prevail over the other. But it is by no means an indifferent matter *which* prevails. On the contrary, significant consequences flow from *whether* the first component eludes the constraints the second component would place on it, *or* succeeds in imposing on the first its control. Durkheim thinks that, if human society is to establish and maintain itself, it is necessary for the second component to prevail over the first, even if not always and everywhere. Such necessity descends from the fact that humans are intrinsically social beings, and their sociality can be affirmed and maintained only if (at the least) the *majority* of individuals in *most* circumstances orient their behavior to expectations expressing their awareness of others and their needs and comply with codes, criteria, and sentiments they share with one another. A given individual can exist and function normally only if he sees himself surrounded by other individuals with whom he ought to peaceably communicate, come to terms, and coexist. This is possible only to the extent that each individual, in considering and addressing the others, abides by salient, long-lasting, demanding constraints on conduct that reflect and affirm the superiority of the second component. Normally, indeed, the interests the individuals share must prevail over those private to each of them. But satisfaction of this requirement must take into account the fact that both components, different and potentially contrasting as they are, inhabit the same reality: the minds of physically separate individuals.

MANNERS OF ACTING, THINKING, AND FEELING

Although Durkheim does not often expressly evoke *homo duplex* and the relationship between the two components of human nature, many aspects of his thought are rooted in the related problematic. Here we address how he deals with this in his main works, starting from his second major book, *The Rules of Sociological Method* (1895). Here Durkheim advances a claim to autonomy for the discipline of sociology, as distinct—in particular—from philosophy and psychology. Basically, he assigns to sociology its own realm of objective reality, constituted by *social facts.*

These facts—or at least the most significant of them—are constituted by the "manners of acting, thinking, and feeling" that a society (broadly understood; it could be a relatively small group) elects as its own and makes binding for the individuals who are part of it, thus securing coordination among their activities and their disposition to pursue common goals. But the existence of these manners, and their actual capacity to affect individuals' feelings, thoughts, and activities, are not natural facts because they are not grounded in biological or psychological mechanisms. They depend on the fact that society confers privileged status on some such manners. Rather than simply inviting individuals to think, act, and feel in a certain way, society strengthens this invitation by means of a "sanction." That is, society more or less explicitly threatens to punish those who act, think, or feel differently, or promises to reward those who act or think in conformity.

Note that the positive or negative consequences of a certain behavior that automatically derive from the nature of it—for instance, the electric shock that results from mishandling a live electric circuit—do not constitute a proper sanction, and the relative behavioral directive ("Turn off the circuit before touching the wire!") does not belong to the realm of the social facts as construed by Durkheim. It is, rather, a *technical* rule. Instead, for Durkheim a proper social fact is a *moral* rule, a sanction-backed prescription whose prototype is a legal norm. For instance, think about the rule that threatens punishment to anyone who kills somebody. Here, the punishment does not follow automatically from the violation of the norm; the threat is only artificially linked by society to given conduct, and actual application of the sanction depends on social—not natural—processes.

Legal norms, however, do not constitute the sole means of attaching sanctions to certain kinds of action (or omissions of action), thus rendering such actions binding for a group. They share that effect with a variety of other sanctioned expectations. Besides formally established and officially implemented sanctions, there are diverse ways of expressing social disapproval of certain acts: invidious gossiping, failing to acknowledge an acquaintance one meets in the street (the English call this "cutting"), blackballing an applicant for admission to a sorority. Likewise, different positive sanctions may reward behavior consistent with social norms: financial success, conferral of good reputation, promotion within an organizational hierarchy, various kinds of honorific titles and trappings.

In any case, it is up to sanctioned, publicly valid manners of acting, thinking, and feeling to orient and discipline the conduct of individuals, and to prevent its being guided exclusively by experiences, preferences, and interests of a private nature relating to what we have called the first, presocial component of their subjectivities. The answer to the question of *which* manners to promote and make binding and *which* to repress or indeed as far as possible render unthinkable constitutes, for Durkheim, the nature itself of the society or group.

Once such answers have crystallized into habits, sets of manners, and shared ways of perceiving, defining, and evaluating reality, which engender congruent flows of everyday conduct, it may be difficult to reconstruct the collective processes that have determined those answers, to identify the social interests meant to be promoted by those manners of acting, thinking, and feeling. (Durkheim for the most part emphasizes the first two elements in this conceptual trio.) It is an intellectual task of sociology to address this problem. Durkheim often performs the task by positing a close correlation between the ways of acting and thinking that a society sanctions and other features of it he generally labels *morphological*. Today we might call them *ecological*, because they refer primarily to the dimensions and the physical character of a society's territory, the size and demographic features (beginning with density) of the population, the pattern of settlement, the kinds of available natural and technological resources, the extent of differentiation into distinctive occupations, the frequency and regularity of the exchanges (if any) occurring between separate parts, and so on.

In such a way, while affirming that society is an intrinsically mental reality—since, as we have insisted, its constitutive elements are primarily manners of acting, thinking, and feeling—Durkheim addresses his analysis to another aspect of society's nature, essentially material in character. The morphological features of a society constitute the substratum of those manners and determine their content—but are as well influenced by them. For example, over time the exchange of different products between parts of society, variously regulated by social norms, influences the material infrastructure, say by way of the construction of roads and the distribution of population settlements over the territory.

Durkheim does not theorize at length about those material elements of society. He largely limits himself to contrasting two morphological patterns: simple (or primitive) versus complex (or advanced) societies. Within the one or the other type, for the purpose of further discussion he subsumes a wide range of historical experiences. This is a serious limitation of his comparative analysis (he believed that comparison is a necessary component of sociological discourse), especially for those who view Durkheim as a theorist of modern society. Modernity itself (as he construes it) is but a late and peculiar historical development occurring in some complex and (more or less) advanced societies, all belonging to the same morphological type, which cannot be distinguished from one another by referring primarily to their respective morphological traits. It is within a different line of discourse, addressing chiefly norms, values, intellectual perspectives, and collective feelings, that (as we shall see) Durkheim makes his own significant contribution to the understanding and criticism of modern society.

Durkheim's first major book, *The Division of Labour in Society* (1893), develops the duality between simple and complex societies, focusing on a fundamental social phenomenon that is somewhat analogous to biological evolution. In the course of the latter, numerous and diverse species develop, and those that evolve later are more complex in their internal constitution than earlier ones. In the same way, developed and advanced societies are internally more differentiated than primitive ones. For example, it is possible to identify within them locales where differing activities are located (in particular, town and countryside); and the individuals occupying each locale are further specialized in their activities, practices, bodies of knowledge, and the techniques they employ.

In short, differentiation and growing complexity are fundamental tendencies of both natural and social development. Why is this the matter in the latter case? Durkheim's own answer to this question is self-consciously proposed as a radical alternative to what we shall call the *utilitarian* answer. This answer belongs to the tradition of liberal social thought that theorizes and celebrates chiefly the economic aspect of modernization, particularly the advances in the division of labor and the ever-growing importance and dynamism of market relationships. In the utilitarian answer, such developments—whose reality and significance Durkheim fully acknowledges—are the spontaneous result of individuals' increasing efforts to pursue their private interests. Basically, to enter more profitable mutual exchanges, individuals develop their respective talents, specialize their activities, and differentiate their products. Thus, according to the utilitarian answer, the pursuit by individuals of their own private interest is from the beginning the very engine of social evolution, and it leads to formation of more complex, differentiated, and changing societies.

Durkheim, however, objects that the individual as the utilitarians view him—an autonomous actor who, to maximize his personal advantage in competition with other actors, specializes and differentiates his activities—in fact could not be said to have existed in primitive societies. There, individuals existed merely on account of the severalness, the physical separateness, of the biopsychical entities making up the society. The "representations" these entertained—that is to say, the images residing and operating within each individual's brain and orienting his actions and thoughts—were largely *collective* in nature, being shared with all the members of the society. On this account, such images were universally perceived as uniquely true and valid, and therefore strongly binding. They induced everyone to carry out similar activities, think the same way, and jointly manage the same practices. These were mainly determined by traditions that the collective representations strongly affirmed, condemning and proscribing innovative ways of thinking and acting.

A society structured in this way was held together—in Durkheim's terms, endowed with *mechanical* solidarity—by the strong resemblance among the representations compellingly entertained by all individuals. The social impact of a given individual's particular representations—his own images of reality, guidelines for action—was thus minimal. In turn, the local units in this kind of society constituted merely the geographically separate segments of an otherwise undifferentiated complex. They were very much alike, and because they were self-sufficient they did not exchange products with each other. At most, the population would gather on ritual occasions to renew and reinforce the hold of collective representations over the entire society.

In this potentially stable context, it simply could not be the case that the phenomenon emphasized by utilitarian thinking—competition among autonomous, self-activating, self-interested individuals—would set on its way the division of labor and the differentiation of society. Such a development could be caused only by the onset of a phenomenon affecting the society as a whole. According to Durkheim, this phenomenon could only be a growth in a society's population rapid and massive enough to upset the pre-existent balance between the survival needs of the population and the environmental resources. The consequent intensification of the struggle for existence within the society could have just three outcomes: extinction of the society as a collective entity, torn apart by conflict and deprived of its subsistence base; return of the population to a size compatible with the traditional balance between needs and resources; or, finally, the start of the process of division of labor.

In this third case, the geographical segments of society identify and activate innovative practices and tools, put to use environmental resources previously left unused (switching, for example, from extensive to intensive use of land, from hunting and gathering of food to agriculture), or specialize each in its own pattern of activities, thus making necessary and possible exchanges among the producers of diverse goods or services. A similar process may take place not between but *within* the parts of society. In a given locality, for example, various segments of the population undertake different productive activities, develop diverse skills, and generate a growing multiplicity of socially differentiated positions, occupations, and professions.

All this diminishes the relevance and prestige of the traditional heritage of knowledge, techniques, and widely shared values, decreasing its impact on the conduct and aspirations of individuals. This erodes the pre-existent *mechanical* solidarity, based on the close similarity between the representations active in the minds of all members of a society, that used to turn it into a tightly fused whole. But such erosion does not *atomize* the society; that is, it does not dissolve it into a huge plurality of parts, each (as in the utilitarian view) totally self-standing and self-regarding. Instead, according to Durkheim, a different kind of solidarity develops, which he labels *organic.*

Organic solidarity rests on the growing differentiation among the component parts of the society and among the individuals making up each part, which renders those parts and individuals highly interdependent, since they can all subsist only by entering into multiple relationships of exchange and mutual service. In this new configuration, the representations orienting the action of parts and individuals also become increasingly differentiated and changeable.

At first glance, this makes plausible the utilitarian vision of enterprising and competitive individuals, each oriented toward private interest and connected exclusively by multiple, diverse, specific, temporary, and ad hoc contractual relationships voluntarily negotiated. But, Durkheim insists, this pattern is plausible only as a product of the division of labor and attendant solidarity (particularly in modern, industrial society), not as a precondition of it. The utilitarian vision is incorrect because it does not acknowledge that individuals may enter into contractual relationships (which are of a private nature) only if a public authority arranges general schemes of contract, establishes how particular covenants can become binding, confers on individuals the necessary legal faculties, and guarantees with its juridical sanctions the respect of the terms of duly negotiated contracts. For these (and other) reasons, Durkheim critiques the liberal position, which would require the state, in modern society, to dramatically reduce its presence, leaving to the market the management of most social affairs.

To return to our starting point: for Durkheim, with the rise of the division of labor, the second (higher) component of *homo duplex* develops in two directions. First, it becomes richer, because each individual's mind can now draw its own contents from an increasingly vast, diverse, and changing universe of images, perspectives, notions, and values. In so doing, this component becomes even more significant than the other, which is still oriented chiefly to natural needs, most of which humans share with other animals. Second, in the mind of each individual the relationship changes between the contents shared with all members of the same society (as these contents become less numerous) and those resulting from membership in a specific group (in particular, an occupation) or from the particularities of biography, the experiences the individual encounters as an increasingly autonomous entity, possessing diverse associations, and committed to the assiduous pursuit of private interest. For this reason, societies with advanced division of labor (modern industrial ones being for Durkheim the most mature historical example) are also characterized by advanced individualization, given the extent to which individuals are allowed—or indeed expected and encouraged—to develop their own personality.

An associated change is the diminished reliance of society on *repressive* sanctions, typically punishment of miscreants and deviants. Such sanctions are a society's natural reaction to behavior that offends widely shared norms and values; they consist in inflicting suffering on those responsible for the offense. However, in the new situation, where such norms and values are rare or are less intensely felt, the most frequent and relevant sanctions are instead *restitutional* in nature. That is, when two parties have undertaken obligations toward one another (generally on the basis of a mutually negotiated contract) and one party discharges its obligations while the other fails to discharge its own, law courts intervene to secure the performance of the undischarged obligations or otherwise compensate the first party for its loss. But this happens only if the aggrieved party resorts to civil court, whereas it is public officials, such as a prosecutor, who typically activate criminal courts, whose concern is punitive sanction. To put it more simply: in *complex, differentiated* societies (those with organic solidarity), recourse to criminal law becomes less frequent than appeal to the remedies afforded by private law. In fact, Durkheim treats the changing relative weight of those two bodies of law as an index of the transition from the prevalently mechanical to the prevalently organic type of solidarity he associates with the advance of the division of labor.

In his *Leçons de sociologie* (translated into English as *Professional Ethics and Civic Morals*), a course he taught many times and known to us from his notes, published some decades after his death, Durkheim suggests that modern society, characterized as we have seen by high differentiation and complexity and by progressive individualization, also tends to acquire a democratic political structure.

The state must be capable of reacting promptly and effectively to the multiple changing needs and opportunities that those same characteristics of the society continually generate, in order to service and integrate the society's constituent members. To this end, the governmental apparatus (which Durkheim construes as an ensemble of arrangements for gathering information about society and deciding on and implementing public policies) must penetrate the social body more deeply and widely, and at the same time open itself to the citizens' inputs (of demand and support, one would say in contemporary political science lingo) by way of their elected representatives.

However, since these needs and opportunities are increasingly produced by developments within the realms of economy and technology, the task of ascertaining and responding to them should be entrusted not exclusively to government (or institutions representing the current distribution of suffrage among political parties) but also to a certain number of "corporations"—publicly recognized groupings of citizens constituted according to the economic sector in which they are employed. This would make immediately visible, at the collective level, the mutual interdependency of the diverse economic activities. Without displacing organizations that serve the private interests of their members, such as business associations and trade unions, the state should grant these corporate bodies the public powers (and sanctioning faculties) they need to both remind the citizens employed within a given sector of their responsibilities toward one another and regulate to the public advantage the relations among the various sectors. The ever more significant effects of economic developments and technological innovations, potentially disruptive for the whole society, can best be managed in this way, instead of abandoning them completely to market relationships (which is to say to the power relations between the various sectors and to the vicissitudes of class struggle).

This proposal expresses *in positive terms* the importance that the concept of norm (*règle* in his vocabulary) increasingly occupies in Durkheim's thinking; the *negative* implications of this preoccupation are embodied in the concept of *anomy*. If social order has to be maintained in any society, the second component of *homo duplex* should include some norms, that is, socially sanctioned expectations that bind and discipline the erratic, centrifugal, and egoistic impulses originating from the other component. Once society has developed beyond its primitive stage (where, as we have seen, norms are collective understandings

universally shared and spontaneously transmitted from generation to generation), the organic solidarity generated by the new conditions requires explicit,
conscious production of specialized bodies of norms.

On this account, as we have seen, Durkheim advocates democracy as a
mechanism for transferring from the political center to society regulatory decisions that correspond to the information flows that, conversely, move from the
society to its political center. The corporations themselves would operate as an
authoritative mediator between that center and society at large. If these requirements are not adequately met, and the need for appropriate social regulation
does not find sufficient response, what results is *anomy*—literally, normlessness.

Durkheim believed that anomy was a tendency inherent in modern society
and would remain so unless the institutional changes he recommended were
enacted. Until that happened, many relevant social processes (particularly, we
have seen, those relating to technology and the economy) would develop in a
disordered way, generating conflict and waste. Besides, modern anomy manifests
itself not only in the absence or inadequacy of explicit normative processes of
a political nature but also in certain aspects of modern culture: the dominant
frames of mind, and the understandings prevailing among individuals about
what society expects of them.

On the latter question, which again connects with the second component of
homo duplex and is of great sociological import, Durkheim has significant and
cogent ideas, best articulated in his third major book, *Suicide* (1897). Here he
suggests that every society (or indeed every group) must induce its individual
members to satisfy three requirements, each in some way indispensable for the
society itself to survive and thrive, but also each to some extent in contrast with
the others.

> Every society should teach the individuals in it to recognize their depen-
> dence on society (which is to say, on themselves collectively), induce them
> to derive from society the most significant guidelines of their own conduct,
> and inculcate in them a disposition, whenever necessary, to sacrifice their
> own interests to the collective one.

> However, it should also exhort individuals to reach a certain detachment
> from society itself, to identify and pursue interests of their own, to express
> their own preferences and seek to attain their own interests by committing

their own energies and assuming responsibility. In other words, individuals should to some extent become autonomous, stand on their own feet, and *not* expect from society comprehensive cues and clues as to how to manage all the aspects of their own existence.

Finally, a society can tackle changing circumstances, surmount unforeseen challenges, and take advantage of unprecedented opportunities only if individuals, within certain limits, are permitted or indeed encouraged to experiment with new thoughts and new activities, venture occasionally beyond established beliefs and practices, and express and promote preferences that are not generally acknowledged and socially validated.

Clearly, as we suggested, there are tensions and contrasts among these dictates, although all of them deserve to be instilled by society; for Durkheim has a strong sense of the complex and potentially contradictory nature of necessary social demands. On this account, he suggests that societies differ (also) because each necessarily emphasizes *one* of these orientations and subordinates the others. The same can be said for the many groups and categories into which a complex society is articulated. Each group or category typically induces its members to respect, in their own behavior, one priority or another among such orientations. One may also expect a given society or group to encounter, in its collective experiences, circumstances making different orientations salient for the duration of those circumstances (for instance, when a society is at war).

SOCIAL REPRESENTATIONS

A further aspect of the complexity of social phenomena that deserves consideration lies at the heart of *Suicide*. As we have seen, the social facts *par excellence*, the sanctioned "ways of acting, thinking, and feeling," are of a mental nature, consisting in "representations" meant to direct and discipline individual behavior, thus enabling ordered cooperation. But such expectations are not self-enforcing. They can carry out their social tasks only through the mediation of the individual subjects themselves; it is up to them whether they actually comply with representations that reflect collective interests and make them prevail over their private ones. These private interests are also part, so to speak, of their mental furniture, but they are not socially sanctioned because they belong to the other component of *homo duplex*.

This "making prevail" is thus a subjective operation, requiring the intervention of the individual's choice and effort, and therefore inevitably contingent. In *Suicide*, Durkheim seeks to identify the social conditions within which it does *not* happen, the reasons a certain number of individuals become (we would say today) "deviant," recurrently turning their backs on this or that social norm. As the title suggests, the book is focused on deviance from the norm that forbids individuals to commit suicide. This norm is forcefully present in all known societies, yet to a varying extent in all of them (and in all of the groups they comprise) it is violated. Although suicide is a rather exceptional and by nature solitary act, it has long been known that there are regularities in its occurrence; different societies and groups have varying (and by and large stable) *rates of suicide*. These regularities are what *Suicide* seeks to detect and explain.

Generally, individuals decide to commit suicide when they are stricken with a deep melancholy or an acutely painful discomfort. This condition may be generated by a number of situations: sharp and prolonged physical suffering, unbearable heartbreak, financial disaster, severe loss of social status. Many individuals across societies and groups experience such conditions, yet only in relatively few cases do these conditions lead to suicide. *Suicide* is a sustained inquiry into the social circumstances in which this happens. It produces findings strongly backed by analysis of statistical data, which at the same time involve a profound, sustained theoretical interpretation. In the book, these two aspects of empirically grounded sociological discourse intersect in an exemplary way.

As we have said previously, every society faces multiple and contrasting requirements, and we can get a fix on the "moral constitution" of each by identifying the priority it posits among them. "Deviance," then, may be said to occur to the extent that the emphasis a society places on a given requirement induces some individuals to ignore others. It may also derive from some individuals making an excessive commitment to a given requirement.

Durkheim develops his argument with reference not only to certain European societies but also to different groups or social categories, whose respective "moral constitution" may again be characterized by those priorities. On these differences depend, in Durkheim's opinion, the suicide rates. For example, the rate of suicide (Durkheim generally calculates it by registering the number of suicides that have occurred in a given population in a given year per 100,000 members of the population itself) is markedly higher in predominantly Protestant societies than in mainly Catholic ones, and among married persons without children rather than those with children. These and other "empirical generalizations" (not Durkheim's expression) may be subsumed under a single "analytical generalization": the suicide rate varies inversely with the social cohesion of categories and groups.

The level of social cohesion, in turn, is low when the moral constitution of a society (or group) emphasizes the second of the three demands that all societies (groups) make of their members. In such a society the individual is expected, and indeed authorized and even urged, to orient his actions and feelings above all to himself, and his own needs and preferences, rather than those of the group. As a consequence of this, his ties with other individuals are not particularly close, intense, and binding. By the same token, the individual is less able to turn to others to bolster his own spirits if his life is exposed to acute discomfort or profound melancholy; consequently, if the temptation to commit suicide presents itself he is at greater risk of yielding to it. Durkheim labels suicides that result from such circumstances "egoistic." Their rate of occurrence, then, is higher for societies and groups rendered less cohesive by their structure and culture—a condition more prevalent in modern than in premodern times.

Paradoxically, a relatively high suicide rate can also be found in social contexts that stress the first requirement, expecting and indeed urging the individual not to focus her feelings and actions on herself but to consider her personal interests as far less important than those of society, and rendering her willing to sacrifice the former to the latter. But should an individual who sets little store on herself experience a condition of overwhelming distress that prompts suicidal thoughts, she will not find a reason to resist temptation in a strong sense of the unique worth and significance of her own personal existence. Durkheim would label her suicide "*altruistic.*" Its rate is *positively* correlated with societal cohesion, which is likely to be higher in primitive societies, where mechanical solidarity prevails.

But also within modern society, cohesion may be high within groups that, going against the grain of the larger society, cultivate and reward in their members a commitment to the priority of group interests over personal ones. Professional members of the military, in particular, learn that in a combat situation their own survival should not be their dominant concern and might have to be sacrificed to the superior interest of the unit or the country. But even outside combat, the resulting diminished sense of a particular individual's relevance can offer little resistance to the temptation of suicide should it be generated by the vicissitudes of existence.

In particular, the relatively high statistical incidence of suicide among officers proves this hypothesis. The rate is higher among senior officers than among officers of lower rank, who in turn have a higher rate of suicide than noncommissioned officers or enlisted men. This excludes a utilitarian interpretation of the phenomenon; suicide probability is higher not among the members of the military exposed to harsh deprivation (typically, enlisted privates) who might consider suicide an escape from those deprivations but among those (typically, officers) who enjoy the advantages their higher rank offers. The military's socialization processes have generated in these relatively privileged individuals a stronger sense of, let us say, their own personal "dispensability," and by the same token, according to Durkheim's data, a higher propensity to suicide.

Finally, Durkheim calls *anomic* the suicide typical of societies that, like modern ones, stress the third requisite, which authorizes or induces individuals to explore situations where no established rules or widely shared criteria of judgment validate and confer a stable, public significance on their activities, their experiences, or their possessions. Such a situation has its merits, putting a premium on individual ability to modify one's own circumstances, discover new resources, and experience new needs and enjoyments. By the same token, the situation tends to discolor the individuals' existence, denying intrinsic significance to whatever they have achieved, since they have learned to consider these achievements only as a means to further ones. Once more, this puts them at risk if, at a certain point, they find themselves under a dark cloud of melancholy and are tempted to kill themselves.

At this point, the individual may no longer find anything that reassures her of her own personal significance, or directs her toward intrinsically valid reasons for resisting the temptation, or toward values and norms by which to justify and orient her existence. Everything turns to ashes, its moral significance having been eroded by the tendency, instilled by society, to consider *all one is and all one has* as merely a bridge to what one is not yet and does not yet have.

Durkheim's evidence suggests to him that this may account for the rather high suicide rate among divorced men. Divorce makes their condition "anomic" because it removes the constraints imposed on men by marriage that constituted moral criteria to orient themselves to. Absent those criteria, divorced men, if they confront an existential crisis, may not find in (again) *what they are and in what they have* enough significance to sustain them and inspire them in the effort required to overcome the crisis.

According to the statistical information on the suicide phenomenon collected and analyzed by Durkheim, modern societies show a particularly high (and growing!) incidence of suicide of the egoistic and anomic types, owing to a deficit of social cohesion in the former case and of normative regulation of expectations and conduct in the latter. Individuals are no longer anchored to strong memberships; their reciprocal ties are weakened, less permanent and demanding, and by the same token less significant and inspiring. In such a condition, they are less disposed, or able, to orient their actions and judgments with reference to criteria that confer an authentic meaning to their ceaseless search for new experiences. The risks associated with this condition account for modern trends in suicide rate as well as in other aspects of the contemporary *social question* (as it was called in Durkheim's generation), characterized not only by the increased divorce rate but more generally by the loosening of family and intergenerational ties.

Durkheim's concern with these phenomena did not induce him, as it did other students and critics of contemporary society, to condemn it and aspire to "restoration" of previous social conditions. He strongly approved of many distinctive aspects of modern society—particularly recognition of individual rights and of democracy, progress toward equality, humanization of penal law, and the growing prestige of science. Moreover, the condition of modern society finds its causes in the continuous advance of the division of labor; thus we see an intrinsic disposition toward change and progress in the growing complexity of modern society. In the vision of the character and tendencies of modernity typical of early Durkheim, the negative aspects of the contemporary conditions are in large measure due to modernity not yet having achieved all its promises, first among them development of the new, organic form of solidarity.

However, Durkheim's later writings, according to many interpreters, reveal a growing perplexity and anxiety, expressed among other things in the previously mentioned proposals for institutional change, chiefly attribution to corporations of public powers of regulation. These proposals express Durkheim's growing awareness that modern society is abandoning ever more aspects of its culture and structure to the spontaneous effects of economic and technological change, whose dynamic is, by itself, not sensitive to or regulated by the appeal of moral values and norms. Essentially, the economic sphere (or, as we would say, the market) places itself openly and arrogantly at the very center of social life at large. Its processes foment the loosening of social bonds, corrode respect for authority and tradition, encourage the individuals' egoism (especially in the form of an uncontrollable greed for material gratification), and place them in unrestrained competition with one another. (This can happen also at the collective level; the frequently conflicting relations between employers and organized workers represent for Durkheim the clash of individual egoisms writ large.)

Moreover, because of their connection to technology and science, economic processes devalue traditional values and knowledge, destabilize everyday existence, and orient it to ever newer experiences, unregulated by shared values and perspectives. Returning to the *homo duplex* theme, one might say in the minds of contemporary individuals the specifically social (collective, public, moral) contents—the second component, as we labeled it at the beginning of this chapter—become less salient and significant, and they find it more difficult to discipline and control the workings of the first component, the mental contents oriented to satisfaction of private needs. As a result, patterns of conduct dictated more or less directly by technical instead of moral rules are increasingly dominant in modern society. Acknowledging this situation evokes in Durkheim what we might call a sense of *pathos*, a growing anxiety about the destiny of modern society and its chances of surviving in the present form. But to some extent this pathos, from a certain point on in Durkheim's intellectual itinerary, is awakened by consideration not only of modern society but of society itself.

In the previous pages we stressed that in the relationship between the individual and society there are three requirements that must be fulfilled, difficult as it may be to establish an equilibrium among them. In Durkheim's thought, this relationship is, or ought to be, markedly asymmetrical; those requirements must find expression in how society addresses individuals, educates them, assists them, and controls them. In many passages of his writings, Durkheim asserts the majesty, energy, and superiority of society over the needfulness, dependency, weakness, unreliability, impatience, and immaturity of individuals. At the same time, his insistence on the necessary superiority of society over the individual conveys his growing anxiety, or again *pathos*, because (as we have already seen) that superiority can only assert itself, when all is said and done, in subjective processes taking place within the individual himself. It is up to him to recognize the superiority of society, to validate the rightfulness of society's claims by submitting himself and fulfilling them. Actualizing the key social facts, the manners of acting, thinking, and feeling, is contingent on individuals, entrusted to their will—one might say their *good will.*

In sum, as Durkheim phrases this point, "Let the idea of society be extinguished in individual minds, let the beliefs, traditions, and aspirations of the collectivity be felt and shared by individuals no longer, and society will die" (Durkheim 1995: 38). Again, this flows from the nature of the norm, which we have suggested is the central concept in Durkheim's thought. That the norm realizes itself in action may be, in the best hypothesis, highly likely, but never sure. It is not an empirical description of actual flows of conduct but a program for conduct, not a scientific prediction but a request addressed to those from whom such flows ought to stream.

This request is, of course, not an impotent one. The norm is a norm because it carries a sanction; it activates compliance by promising the actor positive consequences of action or threatening him with negative ones. Durkheim does not, however, consider the sanction the central aspect of the norm, but rather a symptom of its nature, a signal of the privileged character that society attributes to certain conduct.

In fact, a situation where individuals orient themselves to the norm solely or principally by calculating the probability of advantages and disadvantages they can expect from compliance smacks to Durkheim of rampant utilitarianism and appears to him fraught, to a dangerous extent, with instability and unreliability.

What is required, instead, is for individuals to orient their action on the basis of a strong and persistent sense of moral obligation toward society, inspiring in them willing, uncoerced adherence to society's commands. The norms must activate in them a disposition to transcend and, if necessary, sacrifice their personal interests to those higher and nobler interests of the society or group. The superiority of the second, strictly social, component of *homo duplex* over the first, strictly individual, component, must be motivated by the individual's recognition of the intrinsic validity of the norm, inspired by the particular prestige it possesses for him.

But how can one be sure that the norm does in fact possess such prestige? Is this not, in fact, conferred upon the norm by individuals themselves? On what grounds can one rely on their judgments, evaluations, and preferences—especially in modern, complex, highly differentiated, changing societies—actually to eventuate in conferral of prestige upon the norm? We suggest that Durkheim addresses these queries, loaded with *pathos* as they are, chiefly in his highly original (and controversial) views on religion, put forward in various texts but worked out most extensively and systematically in his last great work, *The Elementary Forms of the Religious Life* (1912).

THE SOCIOLOGICAL ANALYSIS OF RELIGION

Elementary Forms analyzes mainly one religious phenomenon, totemism—a set of beliefs and practices of worship present particularly in Australian aboriginal populations. Durkheim explores it only after having defined the universal phenomenon of religion in general terms. Religion, Durkheim suggests, always postulates an opposition between two realms, the sacred and the profane.

The religious phenomenon is such that it always assumes a bipartite division of the universe, known and unknown, into two genera that include all that exists but radically exclude one another. Sacred things are things isolated and protected by prohibitions; profane things are those to which the prohibitions apply and thus must keep at a distance from what is sacred. Religious beliefs are those representations that express the nature of sacred things and the relations they have with other sacred things or with profane things. Finally, rites are rules of conduct that prescribe how man must conduct himself with sacred things [Durkheim, 1995: 38].

To sum up, *sacred* are the aspects of reality (ideas, objects, practices, places, occasions, roles) conceived as distinct from ordinary (profane) aspects because the former are viewed as markedly powerful and dangerous. On this account, individuals may approach them only in a fearful, respectful, and cautious way, appropriate for evoking and transmitting symbolic meanings, through ritual actions. *Profane* are all other aspects of reality, to be kept at a distance from the sacred ones. Individuals are at liberty to consider and approach them in light of their matter-of-fact features and put them to use in pursuit of their personal, private interests.

Given that these events, things, and processes considered sacred or profane differ significantly among societies, Durkheim wonders why, again, the distinction of sacred and profane is universal, both in the sense that each culture knows it, and in the sense that it divides reality into two juxtaposed and opposing parts.

One element reemerges here: "manners of feeling," which Durkheim mentioned in his early characterization of "social facts" but generally deemphasized with respect to "manners of acting and thinking." In *Elementary Forms*, collective feeling plays a critical role. For Durkheim, there must be an experience—a *universal* experience—that generates in individuals a complex of strong emotions: fear, respect, caution, submission, trust. It is their evoking such emotions that renders sacred particular events, objects, and processes; but the emotions themselves must in turn express a universal experience. This, according to Durkheim, can only be the universal experience of the unequal confrontation between the individual and society.

Briefly: if we call "God" an intrinsically superior reality, with respect to which humans feel inferior and dependent, then "God" cannot but be a symbolic representation of society—its power and majesty. If this is true, religion ceases to constitute, as the Enlightenment thinkers had thought, a complex of misleading beliefs and deceptive, hallucinatory and immature practices, aberrant and unavoidably ineffective: "We can say that the faithful are not mistaken when they believe in the existence of a moral power to which they are subject and from which they receive what is best in themselves. That power exists, and it is society" (Durkheim, 1995: 276–77).

Religion, in other words, represents, evokes, and celebrates in all its myths and rituals, no matter how diverse, a transcendent order of reality with respect to which individuals feel weak, needful, and insignificant, and from which, by embracing those myths and rituals collectively (since religion, unlike magic, is intrinsically social), they expect to receive protection, guidance, inspiration, and strength. Such an order of reality clearly stands in an asymmetric relationship with individuals because again it is at bottom society itself. However, this is a peculiar asymmetry; society itself needs to be continuously regenerated by individuals, by way of the feelings of devotion and submission religious myths and rituals evoke in them. Individuals are at the same time the beneficiaries of society, the addressees of its commands *and* its constituents.

Thus, according to Durkheim, religion engenders and continuously reenacts the superior, collective component of *homo duplex*. The relationship between the two components of *homo duplex* is itself an example of the relationship between the sacred and profane. How does this original (and controversial) understanding of religion bear upon the *pathos* awakened in Durkheim by the intrinsically contingent nature of the relationship between norms and behavior? He gives a complex response to this query. As we have seen, he first emphasizes the intrinsically collective, social nature of religion. Even though some religions construct a direct relationship between the single believer and the deity, all religions emerge from social experience and within social experience, and from a sociological perspective their key effects take place within this same framework.

In short, religion for Durkheim is an ensemble of structures and practices that induce individuals to transcend themselves, projecting them into a sphere of experience where their best faculties and experiences are contemplated and expressed, enabling individuals (together!) to remember and reenact both images of the real (codified in manners of thinking whose prototype is myth) and forms of conduct (codified in manners of acting whose prototype is ritual).

The Elementary Forms of the Religious Life is an inspired work, fervent in exalting the greatness of society. As we have seen, it maintains that God is society and that religion symbolically represents and asserts that priority of the social over the individual on which the very existence of society depends. This is what all mythical beliefs and ritual practices, for all their empirical diversity, affirm and maintain. Precisely for this reason, *Elementary Forms* poses a problem: What about a society—such as the modern one—in which secularization appears to have weakened, privatized, and marginalized the religious experience, and in which egoism and anomy, two phenomena intrinsically hostile or at best indifferent to religion itself, are so widely present?

In various writings apart from *Forms*, Durkheim proposes a solution for this problem: we might say that he "baptizes" egoism itself. He considered modern egoism an immature expression and misunderstanding of a phenomenon that, potentially, has authentic religious significance: attachment of supreme moral value, and therefore of sacredness, to the human being, to the person *as such*. Modern men are egoistic if and to the extent that they attribute such value exclusively to themselves. But expressly modern institutions such as personal rights and freedoms, citizenship, and democracy demand that every individual attribute the same value also to others, their liberty, and their search for self-assertion. Optimally, recognition and validation of the *rights* of each individual should become the *duty* of all.

The realization of such a demand, conveyed to the generality of individuals by modern institutions (beginning with schools and other educational establishments, very dear to Durkheim), may generate strong and widespread feelings of obligation converging toward worship of the idea of the human person. As Durkheim writes, in modern society

a communion of spirits can no longer be focused on specific rituals and beliefs, which are eroded by ongoing developments; thus, nothing remains that men can love and honour in common, except Man himself. Thus man has become a God to men, for they cannot fashion for themselves other gods without lying to themselves. And since every one of us embodies some part of humanity itself, every individual conscience bears within itself something divine, and it is marked by a character which makes it sacred and inviolable for others [Durkheim, 1898: 12].

Thus the human person can and ought to become the supreme sacred object, the center of an expressly modern religion for which man is at once worshipper and deity. Such a religion is of course different from all traditional ones, but it can perform the same functions.

As to the anomic tendencies of modern society, according to Durkheim they can be contained and overcome by appropriate reform of public institutions, and particularly (as we have seen) by attributing specific faculties of enforceable regulation to occupational corporations. One may thus attach to Durkheim the modern label "reformist," for he considered it necessary and possible to deliberately change the structure and culture of contemporary society for the better. It is not clear, however, whether he also thought it likely that such changes would actually be made. In any case, the nature of the reforms he proposed suggests the depth of his concern with what we might call today the sustainability of the social conditions characteristic of his own time.

REFERENCES

Durkheim, Emile, L'individualisme et les intellectuels, *Revue bleue*, 4e série, X, 1898, pp. 7–13, http://classiques.uqac.ca/classiques/Durkheim_emile/sc_soc_et_action/texte_3_10/individualisme.pdf

Durkheim, *The Elementary Forms of Religious Life*, Free Press, New York, 1995.

3 MAX WEBER

German scholar (1864–1920). Born in an upper-middle-class family, undertook a career as a historian of the ancient and medieval economy and as a legal scholar. Conducted research on social aspects of the agrarian economy in Prussia. His studies were so successful that he was offered the chair of political economy first at the University of Freiburg and subsequently at Heidelberg and Munich. Conceives sociology as a discipline committed to creation of conceptual instruments derived from, and oriented to, historical research, and to study of the relationships among various spheres of social life (economy, religion, policy, science, law). Manifests strong political interests, both in his academic writings and in taking part in controversy over matters of internal and international policy.

SUGGESTED READINGS
The Protestant Ethic and the Spirit of Capitalism, Scribner, New York, 1953.
Political Writings, Cambridge University Press, Cambridge, UK, 1994.
Economy and Society: An Outline of Interpretive Sociology, University of California Press, Berkeley, 1978.
The Vocation Lectures: Science as a Vocation, Politics as a Vocation, Hackett, Cambridge, Massachusetts, 2004.
General Economic History, Cosimo Classics, New York, 2007.

FROM THE POINT OF VIEW OF "philosophic anthropology," Max Weber may be said to consider humans as *interpretive beings*, able to manage their own existence only by conferring meaning themselves on the natural and social realities in which they are embedded. The human mind cannot apprehend such realities in full; they are too manifold and ever-changing, too overloaded with aspects, opportunities, risks, chances of misunderstanding, bewilderment, and self-delusion. Consequently, interpreting reality means above all *selecting* certain elements to interpret and leaving out others. The selected elements are then evaluated in light of particular criteria of judgment.

Both activities are of a mental nature and therefore subjective. They play a decisive role in locating individuals within their reality, and keeping the complexity of existence from overwhelming and confusing them to the point of inhibiting thought and action (and survival). The subjective nature of these interpretive processes implies they are basically arbitrary, since it is impossible to present indisputable proof of their validity. Actors, however, are generally not aware of the arbitrary nature of these processes. Acknowledging it would make such selections problematic and reduce their capacity to orient the subject's thought and action consistently and durably. To avoid this, it is necessary, or at least useful, for actors to assume they are orienting themselves according to meanings *read off* reality, even if they are orienting themselves according to what they themselves have actually *written onto* reality.

Essentially, what makes this possible is the fact that such interpretations of reality, though unavoidably subjective, are usually the object and the medium of communication among actors, which renders them *intersubjective.* In other words, they may be (and usually are) shared among a plurality of subjects, making it possible for them to orient and coordinate their acts and thoughts and enabling them to produce and sustain collective visions, judgments, and actions. Moreover, these interpretations are not only transmitted among contemporary actors. They can be shared across generations, resist the attrition exercised on them by the passage of time, maintain their continuity, and structure enduringly the thoughts and actions of individuals and collectivities. In short, because humans are interpretive beings, it becomes possible to locate each individual and other actors within a common reality, taken to be charged with shared meaning and consequently rendered solid and coherent.

For Weber the interpretations adopted by groups (and often sanctioned by means of rewards and punishments in order to assert their shared character) are the ultimate source of such important phenomena as mores, social conventions, norms, laws, and institutions. These are the phenomena that characterize social groups, giving them a collective identity they transmit to, and to an extent impose on, individual members. These phenomena endeavor in various ways to mask the intrinsic arbitrariness of the underlying interpretations, generally by asserting that the validity of their content derives from the intrinsic nature of objects, from the will of transcendental beings, from the "people's spirit" or the "laws of history."

In any case, their subjective nature—along with its corollary, the intrinsic arbitrariness of the interpretations of reality elaborated by individuals and groups—makes a group's internal arrangements of whatever nature inevitably different, and often markedly divergent, from those shared by other individuals and groups. Often this engenders serious misunderstanding and strong conflict between the various units.

As we have suggested, interpretations, in more or less obvious ways, confer meaning on individual experience and structure the coexistence of multiple individuals. Precisely for this reason, individuals cannot view the content of interpretations as the product of random processes. Rather, they mobilize themselves to affirm the intrinsic validity and superiority of their own interpretations and possibly impose them on others, or at least try to prevent others' interpretations from structuring their own existence.

In this sense, diverse interpretations come to constitute distinctive *interests*, or potentially incompatible preferences affirmed and pursued by groups that act in the presence of one another. The nature of such interests, and therefore what is at stake in the social and cultural confrontations they generate, is a question to which Weber replies by affirming the significance of both "material and ideal" interests. He does not assume constant and general priorities between these two kinds of interests but remains open to the possibility that those priorities vary with the situation.

THE "IDEAL TYPES"

This intellectual openness is characteristic of Weber's sociological thinking. He is willing to conceptually embrace highly divergent constellations of material and ideal interests, allowing empirical research to identify the ones that significantly shape a given concrete situation. On this account, social theory is most productive when engaged in formulating typologies, that is, sets of alternative solutions for a specific problem recurring in historical experience. In fact, this is a fundamental task Weber assigns to the discipline of sociology: systematic conceptual elaboration of distinct ways of coping with problems, derived from the enormous variety of concrete historical experience.

For the task to be properly performed, the scientist must first of all envision a small number of solutions with reference to each specific problem. A second requirement is that the solutions be formulated rigorously but abstractly, rendering them relatively indifferent to the concrete details of the multiple and infinitely varied historical conditions they may refer to. It is for this reason that Weber refers to those that make up his typologies as *ideal* types. He consistently reminds the reader that none of them is entirely applicable to any concrete historical reality.

As for the problems to which his typologies are applied, a few examples show the compass of the scholarly horizon on which Weber operates. A typology of cultural solutions may address the question "Given a religion that conceives the divinity as omniscient, omnipotent, and benevolent, how can it justify the fact that often the good suffer and the bad prosper?" (In a nutshell, this is the so-called problem of evil, the object of a branch of theological thinking called *theodicy*.) A typology may also be discerned for the significant solutions to problems of a very different nature, such as "How may a political agency secure the economic resources it considers necessary to perform its own tasks?" For each problem, Weber conceptually elaborates a set of broad and strongly differentiated abstract solutions that, taken as an ensemble, cover the whole range of historically given concrete solutions.

As to the first problem, for example, a theodicy may be inspired by the Manichean vision of a benevolent god, omniscient and omnipotent, who however has to cope with the existence of a "prince of evil" who contrasts his own preferences; or it may theorize that one and the same human soul becomes incarnated several times and in a given reincarnation finds itself in the conditions it has merited by the good or evil it has done in the previous one. As to the second problem, Weber identifies solutions ranging from political agencies financing themselves through the treasure acquired from repeated robberies and acts of piracy to imposition of tribute on a previously defeated enemy country, to the more or less regular levying of resources from the domestic economy through direct or indirect taxation.

It is easier to understand the magnitude of the assiduous conceptual work represented by the Weberian typologies if we take into account certain features. First, Weber devises typologies for diverse life spheres, all historically important and of strong existential significance: law, economy, religion, politics, science, or aesthetic experience. In each sphere, the typology he proposes is rooted in vast historical knowledge, acquired by him sometimes through first-hand specialist research, at other times (and naturally more frequently) by making use of the findings of other researchers. For example, Weber works *autonomously* when he discusses the moral and religious beliefs of various Protestant confessions, demonstrating his knowledge of the primary sources. In other cases, as in dealing with Oriental religions, he relies on translations and secondary literature.

Second, each typology contains few ideal types, but these can lend themselves to further articulation into subtypes and sub-subtypes, incorporating at each level new features that bring the concepts closer to the detail of concrete historic reality. For example, in his important essay "The City" (Weber, 1978), he first differentiates the Western type of city from the Oriental and subsequently distinguishes, within the first type, the ancient Western city from the late-medieval and the modern one, and within the second type the Chinese from the Indian.

Third, in various passages of his most important work, *Economy and Society*, Weber outlines relations between the typologies pertaining to separate spheres. In particular, he argues that the processes typical of the modern economy, centered on the firm and the market, may take place only in the context of particular political, fiscal, and juridical arrangements. He also argues that the initial development of modern capitalism was made possible by the presence of specific, and historically unique, moral attitudes inspired in turn by distinct religious beliefs. In other words, Weber specifies the affinity and compatibility existing among the phenomena typical of a given sphere and those of others, or vice versa the inhibitive effects caused by the lack, in many circumstances, of such affinity and compatibility.

In Weberian analysis, reference to subjective processes alternates with close examination of structures and collective arrangements that to an extent assist or impede those processes, making it likely for subjects to think and act one way rather than another. At this level, however, Weber argues that the solution to *all* social and cultural problems must embody a preference exercised within a single set of fundamental, sharply different, abstractly formulated ways of orienting human conduct within a life sphere, in a historical context. Subjects can indeed orient themselves to any action (or nonaction):

Traditionally, by privileging the modalities suggested by the reverent memory (not necessarily reliable) of the past, assuming that what has always been done deserves repeating and constitutes a valuable, binding model for present action

Emotionally, that is, by giving course to the unreflexive impulses triggered by sensations and sentiments

Rationally, that is, by choosing, from among the *means* available in the given circumstances, more or less expressly, those more apt to achieve their *goals*

But within this third alternative, Weber further distinguishes between

A *value*-based rationality that privileges certain goals and removes others from choice, and

An *instrumental* rationality, disposed to choose not only between alternative means but also between different goals

We may see that, as required by the philosophical anthropology we attribute to Weber, all these are subjective processes. Still, it is not expected that each individual will always and in every situation make a deliberate choice among these modalities of interpretation and orientation. Normally, in a particular aspect of existence, the individual adopts (or adapts to) choices that the group proposes to, and imposes on, him or her as obvious, appropriate, or mandatory. In other words, widely and unproblematically held beliefs, shared definitions of reality, values jointly defined as significant, institutions structuring everyday life—all aspects of a collective context—render individual conduct, in the vast majority of cases, a matter of *routine*, a practice taken for granted, rarely the object of deliberation or contestation.

Let's consider two examples. In the texts in which he discusses political phenomena, Weber explores the "legitimacy" of domination, a condition in which the commands issued by a politically dominant subject (individual or collective) evoke in the dominated subjects an obedience motivated not by fear or by considerations of personal convenience but by a sentiment of moral necessity, of meaningful obligation to obey. Mobilizing the typology of all orientations of action (but omitting, in this case, the difference between value-based and instrumental rationality), Weber claims that such dutiful obedience may be motivated:

Traditionally. Here the command is seen as doing no more than reproducing, in the present, commands issued from time immemorial and on that account deserving of respect.

Charismatically. Here the dominant party is perceived as possessing extraordinary qualities that evoke in the dominated strong feelings of devotion, dependency, and admiration, and a willingness to place themselves at his service by obeying his commands even in breach of tradition.

Rationally. Here the dominant party's commands are seen as deserving obedience because they reasonably apply to the current circumstances, norms, and principles of a general character, valid in turn because they are expressly produced in accordance with binding public procedures.

Even if Weber "typologizes" legitimacy with reference to subjective processes, once established it seriously affects public, objective, practical reality. Within a given political system, both its symbolic and discursive and its material aspects orient the perception of commands by subjects and their reaction to them, thus making plausible, within a given situation, only one particular way of acknowledging (or not) an obligation to obey.

Let's take a second example, again relating to the political sphere (which was of major importance for Weber both intellectually and existentially). The primary modern political institution is the *state*, an ensemble of assets, practices, resources, and arrangements so significant, imposing, and visible that many scholars in Weber's time thought it appropriate to consider "the State" as a self-standing entity, superior to individuals, and as an autonomous protagonist of historical experience. To the contrary, Weber stressed that the state itself, as with any collective reality, exists only *if and insofar as* innumerable subjects (from legislators to judges, from public officers of any kind to taxpayers) systematically orient their respective political activities in a particular way. However, he recognized that at least certain subjects, namely state officials (he was probably thinking of higher-level bureaucrats), were motivated to an extent by serious devotion to the public interest. This motivation reflects their own subjective assumption that the state *is* a reality surpassing individuals, whose distinctive interests should override all private ones—including their personal ones.

IMPLICATIONS OF THE FOCUS ON MEANING

Let us return once more to the fundamental position we have attributed to Weber: humans are interpretive beings, who orient themselves within reality by assigning meaning to given aspects of it. The most significant methodological consequence of such a position is that the student of the facts of human experience should not only *describe* but also *understand* them, referring to the subjective processes that orient and motivate the activities of individuals and thus viewing them as *actions* proper rather than as mere *behaviors*.

Furthermore, within sociological analysis each actor's subjective interpretation of reality must take into account the meanings that orient the actions of other individuals. These others in turn reciprocate by envisaging the first actor's meanings and responding to them positively or negatively. In fact, according to Weber, an individual's action becomes *social action* if and insofar as an actor interprets, more or less expressly and consciously, the activity of other subjects, and vice versa. (It is curious that Weber never expressly discussed the processes of *communication* necessarily involved in these phenomena.)

This position places Weber within the so-called hermeneutic tradition strongly present in his German intellectual milieu, and it raises a serious methodological problem. After all, the student of human affairs is herself, *qua* agent, inevitably engaged in interpretive work, oriented to the meanings *she* attributes to reality, and unavoidably subjective. If this is so, her own scholarly interpretations may, to a greater or lesser extent, bias the meanings she attributes to the individuals she studies and compromise the objectivity of her research results.

We may say that Weber is worried not so much about the threat to objectivity implicit in *selecting* the issues the scholar is interested in as the threat in *evaluating* them. Thus Weber thinks that when passing judgment on the social realities being investigated the scholar ought, as much as possible, to exclude from analysis any *value judgments* and limit the study to *factual judgments*. If he succeeds in doing so, other scholars with different moral and political preferences may also be induced to subscribe to the research results, finding them objectively valid.

In developing this position, Weber self-consciously located himself between two extreme positions within the *Methodenstreit*, a fierce and prolonged dispute among German scholars on the similarities and differences between the human (historical, social, cultural) sciences and the natural sciences. Weber dissociated himself from both extremes, the one stressing the differences between the two kinds of science and the other stressing their similarities.

As we have seen, Weber emphasizes the subjective component of human events. At the same time, he denies that reference to such subjectivities in the context of historical or social research necessarily excludes the objectivity of its results. He also walks a middle path in reference to another aspect of the dispute, arguing that the human sciences, exactly like the natural ones, cannot do without general concepts; rather, these need to be ideal types. As we have seen, sociology in particular must expressly dedicate itself to constructing concepts of this kind.

This scholarly endeavor, however, does not constitute for sociology an end in itself; the ideal types formulated by sociologists are tools for identifying and exploring the historical particularities of human events. They must also make visible the frequency with which certain configurations recur (for example, different ways of connecting the center of a political system with its periphery) and particular regularities present themselves in historical events (to remain within the same example, the periphery's tendency to devise its own "strategies of independence" with respect to the center). Furthermore, Weber believes that the goal of *understanding* human events does not exclude the goal of *explaining* them, even if, in the normal case, such explanations cannot appeal to (or establish) anything like universal "laws."

This position shows again the openness of Weber's sociological thought. It rejects any attempt to claim the priority of a given set of factors in the causation of all historical facts. He is critical of both idealism and materialism as general positions, albeit willing to acknowledge that both may contribute to generating useful, contrasting, but also perhaps complementary explanations of multiple, diverse, and sometimes far-reaching social phenomena. In a late text, for example, Weber first affirms that the *Communist Manifesto* is a work of great scientific significance; but then he proceeds to point out its limitations and errors. In other writings, he claims that Marx's intellectual heritage is still valid, so long as it is taken as a set of hypotheses and not as a dogma able to explain everything.

Compare, for example, the opening phrase of the *Manifesto* ("The history of all hitherto existing society is the history of class struggles") with the beginning of an essay of Weber's: "'Class,' 'Status Group,' and 'Party' are phenomena of the distribution of power within a community" (Weber, 1978: 926). We may notice that, up to a point, Weber agrees with Marx. For both thinkers, the reference to social inequality is important not only for describing the distribution of rewards within a given society but also because such inequality, in all its forms, has to do with *power*. It intervenes in the structure and management of all societies and at the same time tends to generate conflict that may end up changing an existing social structure.

Despite such broad agreement, Weber has a more differentiated vision of social inequality than Marx. He proposes what is often called a *multidimensional* rather than *one-dimensional* vision of social inequality. Besides classes—collective entities resulting from inequalities related to the production and distribution of economic resources—he points to two other inequality-based groupings: *status groups*, resulting from unequal allocation of a radically different resource, social prestige; and *parties*, related to another resource, control over and access to structures and practices connected to organized violence.

Although Weber acknowledges that these different groupings are often in conflict, he does not consider this always to be the case. As opposed to Marx, he does not see in the conflict among the groupings the only "engine of history." Phenomena of a purely cultural nature may cause quite significant historical developments, particularly when there emerge beliefs and values that authorize or extol innovation, or when scientific advances unintentionally make possible new technical capacities.

The Weberian triad of groupings arising from social inequality points out the existence of three forms of power:

Economic power, with respect to which *classes* confront and contend with one another

Political power, with respect to which *parties* (in a broad meaning of the expression) confront and contend with one another

Ideological power, with respect to which *status groups* confront and contend with one another

This position allows Weber to capture theoretically a historically significant kind of conflict largely ignored by Marx. Such conflict does not revolve primarily around the groupings' share of one particular form of power, but around the relative significance of each form, and the comparative significance respectively of class conflict, status group conflict, and party conflict for the total configuration of a given society. In Weber's view, societies differ significantly from one another, among other things, in the priority they assign between the various kinds of power. In the course of historical experience, different groupings take on the protagonist role in social dynamics, acting in the name of dissimilar interests and using diverse strategies. Weber agrees with Marx's idea that, in modern society, classes and their relationships are dominant, while status groups and their relationships are recessive. However, in contrast to Marx he places much more importance on parties as the carriers of specifically political interests.

More generally, Weber attributes to political phenomena much greater relevance and autonomy than does Marx (and Marxists). Marxists see such phenomena as essentially reflecting, to an extent masking and to an extent moderating, what happens in the all-important economic sphere. Weber differs from Marx even more clearly concerning the historical role of religious phenomena. Marx does not devote much attention to religion, considering it a form of "false consciousness," bound to lose ground to other, secularized forms in the context of modern bourgeois society. In contrast, Weber pays much attention to religion in a whole series of sociological essays, published in a scientific journal he began co-editing in 1904 and gathered in three big volumes at the time of his death, plus an entire section of *Economy and Society*. In fact, one may even assert that his reputation as a social theorist still rests largely on those essays, the first of which, *The Protestant Ethic and the Spirit of Capitalism* (1904–1905), is considered by many to be his most significant, and certainly his most original and controversial, contribution to social theory.

Before presenting a brief synthesis of the essay, we may observe that the importance attributed by Weber to religious phenomena once more reflects his view of the human as an interpretive being. It is religion that first allows the individual to locate himself within the universe, to attribute significance to his own existence (and death), and to give a moral and not merely factual meaning to his coexistence with other human beings. Still—and this is a fundamental Weberian assumption, again rooted in his philosophical anthropology—religions perform this task to a differing extent and, most importantly, each after its own fashion, thus in *radically* different ways. Weber thinks such religious diversity has significant and consistent consequences in many other life spheres, including one that at first sight appears markedly mundane and therefore particularly remote from religious concerns. It is precisely the sphere that Marx privileges: the social processes pertaining to production and distribution of wealth.

Weber shares with Marx the idea that the historically variable organization of these processes, and of the group interests that derive from them, may significantly affect and influence various aspects of the religious experience. For example, he holds that all of the great world religions (Judaism, Christianity, Hinduism, Buddhism, Confucianism, Islam) derive significant aspects of their theological content and organizational structure from the interests, including economic ones, of the social groups that were their original historical carriers: the Brahmins for Hinduism, the Arab warriors interested in conquest and plunder in Islam, the begging monks of Buddhism. At the same time, he is far from the Marxist vision regarding the inverse relationship; he thought religious concepts and practices could seriously affect *also* how societies organize production and distribution of wealth. For Marx, we may say that religion is a *dependent* variable in relationship to the economy. That is, religion essentially derives its form and content more or less directly from the way in which economic processes develop in a certain society.

By contrast, in Weberian sociology religion is, or can be, an *independent* variable, a phenomenon exerting a causal impact on processes and structures dealing with production and distribution of wealth. Weber wants to prove this particularly with reference to a historical event to which Marx also attributes major importance: the genesis of modern capitalism.

THE GENESIS OF THE MODERN ECONOMY

Weber does not disagree with Marx concerning the many peculiar, historically unique traits of modern capitalism, in particular the central roles played in production by the private firm, the market, accumulation, profit, competition, appropriated means of production, product innovation, and the contractual relation between employer and employee. (Weber, like Marx, believes that such a relationship entails massive inequality among the parts and generates class conflict; still, he does not subscribe to the idea that such inequality necessarily involves exploitation.)

There is also a considerable amount of agreement between the two with regard to the genesis of capitalism, the conditions that led to the emergence of such a historically unique system. Some of these conditions were strictly economic in nature (among them, the exclusion of subordinate classes from collective resources that had previously provided for their own subsistence) or institutional in nature (the political, juridical, administrative arrangements necessary for private property, private firms, and their market activities). Lastly, Marx and Weber agree that the genesis of modern capitalism has had as its protagonist a comparatively wide social group, a segment of the bourgeoisie that in pursuit of its interests broke through the traditional corporative order, committing itself to new commercial and production practices.

With regard to this group, however, Weber asks a question Marx was not interested in, and his answer ascribes a causal role to a specific religious phenomenon lying outside Marx's purview. Once more, the question reflects Weber's interest in the subjective processes that orient and motivate individual and collective action. He argues that the rising entrepreneurial bourgeoisie could make use of the material and institutional conditions of early modernity and promote new economic structures and processes only to the extent that its daily activities were oriented and motivated in a historically novel way, by what he calls the *spirit of capitalism*. This spirit led individual entrepreneurs to search continuously and intensively for new profit opportunities, and it sustained their unprecedented willingness to accumulate, risk, invest and reinvest, deploy initiative, search for new markets and new products, and adopt whatever commercial and productive practices were conducive to higher efficiency (as well as impose such practices on their employees).

If we refer to Weber's general classification of ways of acting, we may see the new entrepreneurial bourgeoisie as rejecting the traditional and the emotional ways, adopting instead the rational one—a mode that entails (in this case) continuous selection among different *means* of economic activity in light of their capacity to maximize the *goal* of profit accumulation.

This criterion should not be conflated with sheer greed, to what used to be called "the execrable hunger for gold" that has always been practiced by men and criticized by moralists. The difference is that the capitalist spirit made the assiduous search for profit a *moral duty* for the entrepreneur; it demanded an impersonal, systematic, and untiringly objective commitment to acquisition, with respect to which the search for immediate gratification (new consumption experiences, a more comfortable and leisurely lifestyle) represented a temptation to be avoided as an obstacle to moral righteousness.

To sum up, the entrepreneur must continuously invest and direct toward growth all resources at his command, from strictly personal ones—such as his own time and energy—to more objective and external ones, such as the capital needed to start a factory as a material ensemble of machinery, supplies, manufactured goods, and personnel. Such duty must dominate the entrepreneur's existence; its performance must constitute a goal in itself. In pursuing it, the entrepreneur has a chance to prove he has authentic moral qualities: industry, mindfulness, punctuality, inventiveness, adaptability, reliability in interpersonal relationships, persistency, and responsibility. At stake in the individual's entrepreneurial activity, therefore, is demonstration of his own ethical quality.

How could such a spirit have been born and become accepted by a sizeable number of individuals in the historical environment of early modernity, where traditional religion considered morally despicable, or at least suspect, such pressing devotion to the utterly worldly goal of acquisition and profit? Weber agrees with many scholars that removing such religious impediments to a new personal morality was one of the historical tasks performed (intentionally or not) by the massive religious innovation represented by the Protestant Reformation. Nevertheless, he denies (and in this he differed markedly from established views) that Luther's religious vision had played a decisive role in this regard. Luther certainly invested with spiritual and moral meaning the individual's occupation/vocation/ profession (his *Beruf*); but he conceived of it in traditional terms. He thought that by performing his *Beruf* in the conventional, stylized manner sanctioned by tradition, each individual would, as it were, fill the specific slot assigned him within the orderly ranks of the corporate system. If the *Beruf* in question was a craft or commercial position, he should dutifully abide by rules of conduct designed to keep at bay innovation and competition and to maintain solidarity among those occupying a given rank.

According to Weber, rather than in this Lutheran understanding of the moral and religious significance of the *Beruf*, the spirit of the new entrepreneurial groups had its religious roots in the vision of another great reformer: Calvin. According to the Calvinist dogma of *predestination*, God by his own inscrutable decree has assigned from all eternity, to each individual, an inescapable fate either of salvation or of damnation in the afterlife. Weber argues that those adhering to this belief inevitably experience nagging anxiety regarding their own personal destiny as saved or damned, a destiny they cannot know or modify. (It should be remembered that in Calvinist theology there is no room for sacraments or other ritual pathways to grace and justification.)

Individuals holding such a belief may be induced by it to shape their whole life conduct, beginning with its occupational aspect, as an untiring, sustained, rationally oriented attempt to prove to themselves that they *are* after all destined for salvation. Such an undertaking makes sense at a purely psychological level, in spite of its lacking any theological warrant. It commits the individual to a historically novel form of *asceticism*, not to be pursued, as it was by medieval monks and other "religious virtuosos," as a retreat from the world and its mundane concerns. On the contrary, this belief must be adopted and pursued within the world as it is. It considers one's occupation, the pursuit of one's mundane everyday tasks, not as the performance of a fixed, traditional script but as an opportunity to prove one's moral mettle, by performing one's duties in as selfless and exacting a manner as possible. Thus understood and practiced, such *worldly asceticism* turns each believer into an instrument of the superior glory of God.

Weber's argument to this effect is complex, tortuous, and on various points questionable. The controversy that immediately arose on publication of the essay on the Protestant ethic induced its author to intervene several times, always to re-affirm his thesis. This, as we have seen, is in open contrast with Marxist thinking, for it imputes to a theological component of such an expressly religious phenom-enon as the Reformation a critical role in the formation of the capitalist spirit, and to the latter in turn a critical role in the development of modern capitalism.

Moreover, in the vast series of essays following *The Protestant Ethic*, Weber tried to offer a *counterproof* of his argument. He pointed out that in some his-torical situations (such as those present for centuries in the Chinese empire) there existed material and institutional factors that could have allowed modern capitalism to emerge. However, the prevailing ethical views made impossible the development of worldly asceticism, *therefore* the emergence of the spirit of capitalism, *therefore* the formation of an entrepreneurial group that could con-sider accumulation and profit morally worthy and dignified goals, and *therefore* the genesis (and the later triumph) of anything similar to modern capitalism.

Of course, this did not deny the fact that in a subsequent period, in some Asian countries, the traditional commercial and productive structures were more or less rapidly subverted by the imperious capitalist dynamic, and the latter was subsequently pushed forward also by locally grown, new entrepreneurial per-sonnel. *The Protestant Ethic* concerns the *genesis* of modern capitalism, not its subsequent expansion.

In fact, according to Weber, after establishing itself in the original histori-cal locale of early modern Europe, capitalism has been able to dissociate itself from its original spirit. From a certain point on, the objective requirements of the functioning capitalist system automatically forced entrepreneurs to adopt rational and innovative life conduct if they were to survive in the competitive process. It freed itself even more clearly from the religious beliefs and practices that had played a decisive role in its genesis. To use Weber's lapidary phrase, "The Puritan [here, a synonym for "Calvinist"] *wanted* to work in a calling; we are *forced* to do so" (Weber, 1953: 181).

In his sociology of religion (or more precisely of *religions*) Weber also deals with another large question: What distinguishes Western civilization from other great civilizations? He sees the specificity of Western historical development in the extent to which (and the intensity with which), in the most diverse fields, it systematically induced individuals and groups to adopt distinctively rational ways of thinking and acting. For centuries, starting with ancient Greece, Western culture and institutions have privileged the search of consciously and expressly rational ways (that is, aimed at optimizing the relationship among means and goals of action) to generate and transmit knowledge, practice the arts, produce wealth, exploit natural resources, make war, settle civil controversies, punish antisocial behavior, and construct and manage institutional arrangements of various kinds. In such ways, Western culture has greatly increased human mastery over nature and the ability of humans to take control of significant aspects of their own existence.

Precisely this enabled the West, from a certain point in its history, to impose its rational superiority on other civilizations and cultures, and force other parts of the world to adopt, to a lesser or greater extent, ways of interpreting and handling the most disparate aspects of existence that had originally been uniquely Western. Paradoxically, one might say, the peculiarity of the West is having been the terrain where ideas and institutions were originally developed and tested. Subsequently they asserted themselves *universally* on account of their practical efficacy (*not* of their moral worth, the judgment on which, according to Weber himself, is intrinsically too value-laden to be part of scientific discourse).

POLITICAL POWER

In developing his thesis on the peculiarity of Western civilization, Weber parallels his argument on the economic dimension, at the center of his study of religions, with one on the political dimension. The West is also the original *locus* of two great experiences related to constructing and managing institutionalized political power (the form of power, he insists, that is ultimately grounded in organized violence): the city (classical and medieval) and the modern state. The second is by far the more important, because the state, first developed and established in the modern West, has subsequently established itself in the rest of the world as the dominant political institution of modernity. Of course, in dealing with the state Weber inserts it in a wider typology of political bodies among which it stands out because of the peculiar, rational orientation of its structures and processes.

In early modern Europe, the princes holding political power in certain centers succeeded in seizing a monopoly of legitimate violence over larger and larger territories. They did so despite the resistance of other centers, imposing on these their own superiority while at the same time affirming their own autonomy vis-à-vis both the Church and the Empire. Once each state, with varying timing and modalities from case to case, acquired sovereignty (internal and external), it engaged in an increasingly rational increase and management of its own power and might through a purposefully designed and progressively centralized political, military, fiscal, judicial, and administrative apparatus. Weber's analysis of these processes (one of his most significant contributions to modern social theory) constructs an elaborate ideal type of *bureaucracy* within a broader typology of ways in which a political center may establish and administer domination over a large territory. For him, bureaucracy constitutes a uniquely effective ensemble of arrangements for performing such a task continuously, systematically, and efficiently, and for integrating expressly political processes with administrative ones.

Within a typically bureaucratic administration, personnel act within structures designed according to a more or less pyramidal model in which authority flows from the top down, or from center to periphery. This allows it to conduct administrative and political affairs as much as possible in a coordinated and uniform way, on behalf of expressly political interests: the security of a given state in its relationships with others, and preservation of both public order and the structures of social power within the society.

The state's commitment to these interests (together with such other aspects as frequent employment of *law* as a political instrument) confers on it an expressly rational-legal legitimacy. It is constituted and operates as a machine, in a purposive, dynamic, and yet relatively predictable (and programmable) manner. It pursues interests relevant to the generality through increasingly public processes: legislation, periodic changes in the composition of the political elite, advancement of officials along hierarchical career tracks, prohibition to officials of pursuing private advantage in their professional activities, arrangement and control of a predictable flow of resources from the economic system to the political-administrative through taxation, etc.

In the course of this development, the state acquires further features, again originally Western:

It frames and adopts a constitution.

It claims a socially and culturally vast entity, the nation, as its constituency and as the original source of its sovereignty.

It involves a growing portion of the population in military activities.

It allows formation of a public sphere and of competing political parties, which make critical inputs into state policies.

It awards the highest political offices to a party that, in competition with others, achieves the majority of votes but must expose itself to the critique of the opposition and periodically put into question its leading position.

It bestows on citizens rights of variable extent and content.

It manages politically and administratively a range of increasingly diverse social affairs.

It collects updated information on many conditions of actual or potential public relevance.

It regulates multiple social activities by means of a larger and more complex apparatus, operating on the basis of ever more diverse bodies of scientifically grounded knowledge.

These processes, however, do not invariably yield their expected positive effects. They interfere to a varying extent, in the name of political and administrative rationality, with the economic rationality of the market. They overload the state machine, rendering it more expensive and less efficient. Also, in forming and implementing public policies, the interests of various administrative bodies sometimes prevail upon more expressly political interests. The whole bureaucratic apparatus, it sometimes appears—despite the intent of the original design—is not particularly open to innovation or devoted to efficiency and rationality but instead appears particularly attached to its own privileges. Officials are not always informed and efficient in pursuing the goals assigned to them by political personnel. Their work is dominated by a "bureaucratic" mentality, in the common, disparaging meaning of the term. That is to say, administrative officials often act tardily and slowly, and they use their professional knowledge of rules and of factual circumstances to increase their own discretionary power, shielding it from the political and juridical agencies intended to control and limit it.

These phenomena, as Weber saw them in his own time, do not gainsay the intrinsic superiority of the *state* as a way to build up and manage political power. Still, they worried him, particularly as they revealed themselves in contemporary Germany. Bureaucratic modalities of administration impose themselves, in the modern world, far beyond the political sphere; they establish themselves within firms, universities, hospitals, churches, trade unions, parties, mass media, and various other social groups. The panorama of modern society increasingly reveals the massive, hegemonic presence of organized entities, bureaucratically managed in order to secure their rational, predictable, and efficient functioning, but not always able to attain this goal.

According to Weber, the phenomena in question, though originating in the West, endanger *other* precious particularities of the Western civilization, chiefly by leaving less and less space for the autonomy, initiative, and responsibility of individuals in their own chosen pursuits. With an eye (a worried eye) on this phenomenon, although conscious of profound social and moral reasons for the growth of socialist movements, Weber feared the prospect of their establishing through political means a collective (unavoidably bureaucratic) control over industrial firms and their market operations. Such reforms would compromise one of the few remaining grounds on which Western individualism could still affirm itself (albeit with growing difficulty, given the increasingly bureaucratic processes of management within the larger industrial firms themselves): the competitive market, which systematically registers and rewards the individual's capacity to risk, innovate, and compete.

Weber believed something of this sort was happening also in the political realm. In the contemporary world, the possibility of authentic statesmanship, capable of conceiving and pursuing great political projects, within individual states or in their mutual relations, has come to depend on the operations of the representation system, the plurality of the parties, their competition in the public sphere, their ability to express public opinion. Two phenomena, however, make it difficult for such statesmanship to emerge.

In the first place, even those politicians who attain the political summit might find their policies blocked or perverted by the state's bureaucratic apparatus. Civil servants who supposedly dedicate their professional activities to the objectives chosen by the political leadership under its own responsibility, and who put their expertise and technical competence at the service of that leadership, instead often use them to pursue the interest of their own caste and preserve their personal attachment to established norms and routines—the *status quo*.

Second, the competition within and between parties for selection of leaders by appealing to their respective constituents or to the citizenry at large is often distorted by the role played by the parties' own bureaucratic personnel. They control the party's resources, distribute patronage within it, and shape the appeal to the electorate. In doing so they often seem to attribute the greatest priority not to attaining the party's official goals but to preserving their own positions and the organizational well-being of the machine they run.

In such a panorama, rendered particularly worrisome by Weber's pessimism about the political resources of Wilhelmine, and subsequently of Weimar, Germany, we might find the explanation for his dramatic emphasis, particularly toward the end of his life, on the necessity of a *charismatic* leader. This would be a politician with a strong, passionate political calling, capable of evoking credence, loyalty, and commitment to expressly political goals among her followers strictly on the basis of personal talents, especially oratory, and of committing them to the attainment of political goals of her own choosing. Only such a leader, Weber insisted, would be able to neutralize the sullen resistance of the bureaucratic apparatus, at the party and state levels, and confront the ultimate challenge of modern politics: securing and maximizing a state's might within the "anarchical" context generated by the competition among many sovereign states.

All in all, Weber views modern society with considerable anxiety. First of all, the dominant tendency (originally developed within Western civilization) to rationalize all social processes relentlessly marginalizes and downplays alternative ways for the individual to perceive reality and orient himself within it—in particular, ways inspired by tradition or expressing strongly held values. In other words, the particular form of rationality characteristic of the West, oriented to mastery over natural and social reality, obscures alternative forms, such as those represented by classical Chinese culture, where the individual is urged to attune himself to the demands and potentialities existing within a given natural or social order, listening to and respecting its natural rhythms and harmonies, instead of arranging and rearranging it in the pursuit of personal or collective interests.

Modernity still leaves room for individuality and, on this account, weakens the hold of social bonds, the appeal to interpersonal trust, and feelings of solidarity. In particular, both the market (which can still reward individualistic attitudes and behavior) and formal organizations induce participants to treat one another either as means or as obstacles to the pursuit of one's advantage. In turn, as we have seen, the tendency toward bureaucratic management of all manner of collective activities threatens to narrow down the cognitive horizons and ambitions of individuals, turning everyone into an insignificant, anonymous cog within larger and ever more self-activating machinery.

Note that in Weber's view the negative aspects of such a vision of modernity go hand in hand with its acknowledged merits: the space it originally created for individual autonomy, the rationalization of social processes, the encouragement of science. Once more, his overall judgment on the great historical event of modernity turns out to be distinctively "open"—to the multiplicity (and contradictory nature) of the values to which historical judgment may appeal, and to the inescapable contingency of possible future developments.

REFERENCES

Weber, Max, *Economy and Society*, University of California Press, Berkeley, 1978.

Weber, *The Protestant Ethic and the Spirit of Capitalism*, Scribner, New York, 1953.

4 GEORG SIMMEL

German philosopher (1858–1918), whose work deals also (mostly in writings originally published as essays) with a large number of issues relating to sociology. Simmel defines sociology's scientific mission in a rather original way, as a study of sociohistorical phenomena focusing on the *forms* taken, in pursuit of the most disparate interests, by the interaction among individuals and collectivities. His academic career was remarkably slow, as he met with hostility from many established academic figures. He was, however, rewarded with broad popularity as a public intellectual. He had strong aesthetic interests and paid special attention to the expressive dimension of his writings and lectures.

SUGGESTED READINGS
Sociology: Inquiries into the Construction of Social Forms, Brill, Leiden, Netherlands, 2009.
The Philosophy of Money, Routledge, London, 2004.
Conflict: The Web of Group Affiliations, Free Press, Glencoe, Illinois, 1964.

O NE MAY CONVEY the image of human beings that inspires Georg Simmel's sociological thinking by recalling a sentence in which Kant (the great German philosopher of the 18th century, whose writings were widely and extensively revisited and discussed in Simmel's own time) attributes to the human being an *ungesellige Geselligkeit*, an "unsociable sociability."

Explicitly or implicitly, this characteristic insight echoes throughout Simmel's writings. He sees individuals as always entering and entertaining relations, finding themselves necessarily, to some extent and in some manner, involved with one another. As they do so, however, they always maintain a certain distance and reserve vis-à-vis others, seeking to acquire and preserve some amount of autonomy and independence, and a greater capacity than their counterparts to themselves determine, or at any rate affect, the content, duration, limits, and course of their relations. Strong as one subject's need for attachment to another may be, these feelings must always be tempered by an aspiration to remain self-standing and control the other subject, or at least moderate its impact on oneself within the relation. On this hangs, for each individual, nothing less than the ability to experience individuality, and to express and enjoy it in his or her own conduct. The individual risks losing such ability if she too closely and unreservedly identifies with the group to which she belongs and whose interests or will she submits to—an eventuality that of course would favor the *other* members' similar and contrasting interests.

On the one hand, this view reflects the keen sense Simmel's own thought (beginning with its philosophical components) reveals for the complexity, ambivalence, and contradiction that pervade reality in all its aspects. On the other hand, the view is articulated in a particularly creative and insightful manner in his sociological writings. Indeed, the fact that they largely consist of essays closely exploring several distinct themes (some of which we consider below) may reflect Simmel's intent to show how widely and diversely those aspects affect the nature of social experience. Mostly, his essays discuss the tensions and contrasts characterizing that experience, and in doing so they display one of Simmel's favorite rhetorical devices, his emphasis on paradox. This is often evident even in how he announces the topic of a given essay, as if each time he sought to shake up the reader's preexisting, commonsense ways of understanding the topic under consideration.

Consider some examples. Simmel states the theme of an impressive "Excursus on 'the Stranger'" by characterizing such a person not as "the wanderer who comes today and goes tomorrow" but as "someone who comes today and stays tomorrow." In another essay, he identifies two contrasting tendencies within the phenomenon of fashion: on the one hand an individual follows fashion to distinguish herself; on the other hand, she does so by conforming to the preferences of those others considered "fashionable." Simmel conceptualizes exchange—which he considers the economic activity *par excellence*—as chiefly expressing not the individual's intent to *acquire* something she does not have (for exchange shares such intent with stealing, begging, and receiving gifts) but her disposition to *give up* something she has, though naturally with an eye on something not possessed. Also, in the second sentence of the opening paragraph of his essay on conflict, Simmel himself calls "paradoxical" the question of whether "struggle [between individuals or groups] constitutes a form of association" (Simmel, 1950: 13), but he answers the question affirmatively. Finally, in one essay he points out "the psychological antinomy that, on the one hand, we are attracted by what is like us, and, on the other, by what is unlike us" (216).

Simmel's attention to the more or less hidden potential for conflict within social relations, and to the fact that *Ungeselligkeit* (unsociability) constantly accompanies and counterbalances the human being's natural *Geselligkeit* (sociability) and his penchant for what one might call "counterintuitive" utterances, enliven his sociological discourse, which has other literary virtues as well. One of them, which led an observer to call him "a philosophical squirrel," was particularly evident in his lecturing style but also manifest in his writing. Simmel liked to surprise his listener or reader by giving his argument a sudden new twist, illuminating unforeseen facets of his topic, and applying his insights to a variety of aspects and contexts.

In this way, in his sociological production Simmel explores in depth the theme of how social relations are constituted and managed, and how they develop and end. He deals with relations on the scale of individual interactions as well as collective ones, sometimes as large and persistent as whole nation-states. His fundamental intuition is that social relations necessarily involve a "reciprocal effect" (*Wechselwirkung*), for the *ungesellige Geselligkeit* itself affects all parties in the relation, orients, and motivates each unit involved. However, this phenomenon alone need not always destabilize the relation, deprive it of significance, or threaten its existence. Rather, it can induce the parties to renegotiate the terms of their engagement, to emphasize its shared components and the mutual satisfaction they produce rather than those engendering contrast.

Let us examine how Simmel presents a plain, mundane example of this process. Imagine that two people decide to visit an art museum together. It may happen that they differ in their aesthetic tastes and preferences; one may desire to explore Calder mobiles, while the other is a devotee of ancient Asian art. This does not necessarily entail that in the course of the visit they will choose separate itineraries, lose contact with one another, and find themselves unable to share the resulting aesthetic experience. If the museum contains the works of artists appreciated by *both* visitors, they may enjoy visiting them *together*, focusing the experience on those works and sharing the aesthetic stimuli they receive from them.

If we stay with this example, things may easily become complicated. The happy outcome we have envisioned is possible if one party appreciates artists A and B, and the other appreciates instead B and C. Here, all that needs to happen to generate shared gratification is for these two to communicate to one another their preferences and subsequently to focus their museum visit on B, bracketing

A and C. However, suppose on another such visit a third party joins them. This person, as it happens, shares an exclusive aesthetic preference with each of the others—but he shares A with the first party and C with the second. At this point, Simmel remarks, it is not possible for the three visitors to enjoy a pleasurable, shared aesthetic experience.

FORM AND CONTENT

This difference between what may happen respectively in a relation *à deux* and in one *à trois* points out one of Simmel's significant sociological arguments. The difference between the two situations, concerning the probability—indeed, the possibility itself—of what he calls a "unification of feelings" between parties, is a function of the *number* of individuals involved. Simmel insists that the number of participants is a strictly *formal* property of the relation. It is formal first in that the number of the parties involved affects in a relatively similar way quite different situations in which two or more parties try to coordinate their activities. The parties may be single individuals or large (even very large) groupings; they may share occasional and brief, or persistent, experiences, which may be (as in the case above) aesthetic or markedly material (economic, military, etc.). Their historical contexts may also vary greatly.

In the second place, the number of participants is a formal property of the relation because what happens (or does not happen) in it as a function of the number involved does not constitute part of the content of the relationship they pursued in establishing and managing it. The three characters we just envisaged do not go to the museum *to experience being a trio*. Rather, Simmel insists, the mere fact of their visiting the museum *à trois*, rather than *à deux* (*à quatre, cinq*, or whatever), makes it more or less likely, or indeed possible or impossible, for them to share certain experiences (whatever those might be) and may to some extent have an effect (positive or negative) on attainment of the interests they pursue in visiting the museum (especially if we assume that, for instance, their sharing and communicating about an aesthetic pleasure increases it, making it more conscious and intense).

The distinction between the *form* and the *content* of social relations is very important for Simmel, who employs it to justify the existence of sociology as a distinct discipline. So understood, sociology would establish its own autonomy from other disciplines much more established in the German academic context of Simmel's own time, which did not allow any space to sociology, although some of those disciplines shared with it a generic concern with social and historical reality. For instance, law and economics also study social events and structures and examine, each within its own realm, relations between individuals or between collective units. But, Simmel observes, in doing so both disciplines characterize those relations, classify them, and interpret them, with respect to their *content*, that is, the interests pursued in such relations, the social needs they satisfy, and their contrasts. Sociology, instead, should examine juridical or economic relations (among others) by attending to the diverse *forms* they assume. Such forms may appear irrelevant from a purely juridical or economic viewpoint; nonetheless, they may seriously affect the unfolding and outcomes of those relations. They may, for example, make it more or less likely that conflict will arise between a relation's participants.

Let us consider again the *number* of the parties involved in a relation, beginning with a relation *à deux* with whatever content—a dyad, Simmel calls it. Like all relations, any dyad (whether a pair of friends, a couple of lovers, two firms involved in a joint venture, or two allied nation-states) has a complex dynamic generated by *ungesellige Geselligkeit*. If the dyad is to persist, a balance must be found between each party's acknowledgment of the other's interests (both those they share and those exclusive to each) and its own interest in maintaining some degree of autonomy, limiting its own costs, and determining to a self-satisfactory extent what activities to carry out together.

Furthermore, the dyad as such has peculiar features, including "intimacy," as Simmel characterizes its tendency to become the site or vehicle of emotions, interests, and purposes with which parties normally do not endow any other relations. Above all, the dyad is constitutionally "fragile," for its continuity and its very survival depend totally on the ability and disposition of each party to remain within the relation. In turn, the dyad's intimacy and fragility normally make it the object of the parties' special attention and concern, and they evoke in them particularly intense expectations and feelings. (Hence the suddenness and sharpness with which, say, the relations within a marital couple, once "gone sour," may degenerate into intense hostility between the spouses.)

At the same time, let us imagine that at some point a dyad (perhaps to reduce its fragility) opens itself to a new participant and becomes a *triad*. Here, again, we witness the significance of the *ungesellige Geselligkeit*. On the one hand, the original relation may be strengthened because an indirect bond resulting from the relation of A and B to C is added to the direct bond between A and B. For example, the birth of a child may enrich and deepen the relationship between the parents. However, it may instead weaken the relationship, sooner or later, by awakening jealousy between them. More generally, each party's *Ungeselligkeit* in a triad may induce it to assert its own superiority and autonomy within the relation, by turning the third party into a special ally, negotiating with it in order to box the other into a corner or assign it an inferior position.

In principle, Simmel observes, each member of a triad, operating as a third party, may adopt various strategies allowing it, in this capacity, to increase its own autonomy and control. In particular, he considers how a third party can behave vis-à-vis the others when a contrast exists or emerges between them. It can take upon itself to terminate or moderate such conflict by acting as a *mediator* (that is, as a *link* between the contenders, allowing each to learn and evaluate the other's complaints, claims, and intents, and negotiating an accommodation) or as an *arbiter* (to whom the contenders confer the authority to settle their differences by his own decision). The third party may also become a *tertius gaudens*, that is, take advantage of the conflict between the two contenders—for instance, watching them waste their own energies and resources in opposing each other, while leaving intact (and comparatively increasing) its own resources.

Finally, the third party can adopt a *divide and conquer* strategy; that is, it can purposefully (though preferably in a concealed manner) occasion friction and struggle between the other two with resultant waste of their energies, rendering both unable to challenge—either singly or jointly—the third party itself, which can thus establish its own superiority within the triad.

Simmel gives numerous examples of these configurations, again drawing them from diverse social experiences at various levels: the interpersonal one (as in the case mentioned above, addition of a child to a conjugal dyad), relationships between collective components of the same system (for example, the gains accruing to the English monarchy from the war of attrition between the great aristocratic houses during the War of the Roses), or confrontations and power games between sovereign states. The fact that the distinctive triad dynamics manifest themselves in situations so diverse in their *content* allows him to emphasize the significance of a sociological discourse focused instead, as we saw, on the *form* of the relations in question.

Here we will not take up Simmel's further arguments for the possibility of establishing sociology as an autonomous discipline that conducts sustained analysis of the formal aspects of social events. But we may mention one metaphor clearly expressing this conception: he suggested viewing sociology as the study of the *geometry* of social relations. The properties of the triangle are the same for the most diverse kinds of triangular objects, be they pizza slices or land holdings—and this is true for all geometrical figures. Thus Simmel assigns sociology a daunting scholarly project: to identify and classify the various shapes (concrete or more often metaphorical) social relations and groupings may take, specifying the constitutive properties and developmental tendencies of each shape. He lists various social phenomena that manifest themselves, more or less openly and consciously, in social contexts differing widely in dimension, duration, and historical circumstance: domination, subordination, cohesion, division of labor, exchange, shared defense and attack, party formation, and many others. He suggests that each such phenomenon has a logic of operation and tendency of development of its own, and it confronts participants with recurrent alternatives that again sociology, according to Simmel, must identify, analyze, and compare.

Simmel never systematically attempted to carry out this "geometrical" program; it required a willingness to undertake systematic analysis that he lacked, at least in his sociological writings. (Subsequently, other German sociologists, among them Alfred Vierkandt and Leopold von Wiese, pursued that program with varying success.) The closest Simmel comes to this sort of analysis is in his *Soziologie* (1950). This book, despite its systematic-sounding title, is actually a collection of essays addressing loosely related themes, although mostly expressing a coherent inspiration. Many of them, furthermore, constitute sound illustrations of the Simmelian program's ability to produce valid, penetrating, often striking insights, and in their internal structure they approach systematic rigor.

We have already drawn on some of these essays, gathered in *Soziologie* into the section "Quantitative Aspects of the Group" (1950: 87–180), in particular comparing the dyad and the triad. Now we briefly draw on another essay whose very title echoes the geometrical metaphor, "The Intersection of Social Circles," though its excellent English translation prefers "The Web of Group Affiliations" (1964). Here Simmel imaginatively employs spatial imagery to explore a highly significant aspect of modern society: the growing autonomy of the individual. He does not interpret this phenomenon as entailing development of an atomized society, where each individual stands separate from all others, in a posture of sovereign detachment and rejection of commonality. Even in modern society, the human being continues to show essential sociability, but this undergoes, so to speak, a particular alteration, revealing new aspects of *un*sociability.

Within the process of modernization, individuals do not cease to belong to groups or establish relations and construct social circles. What changes is how the individual's resulting multiple memberships relate to one another within the broader social context. Basically, in premodern societies, particularly those more remote from modernity, the individual finds himself assigned a number of membership positions within a set of *concentric* circles: a single fundamental datum (typically, his social location at birth) determines not only the family, the larger kinship group, and the neighborhood where he belongs but also with whom he will share educational and work experiences, religious beliefs and practices, leisure activities, political commitments—in short, the relationships to broader society. Here, then, sociability finds expressions in diverse affiliations, but many of the related experiences involve a given individual with a relatively narrow set of predictable associates. Under these circumstances, each individual's conduct, in its various aspects, is rendered "transparent" to his associates; it can be observed and monitored closely and continuously, evoking reward or reprimand and punishment according to consistent, generally subscribed criteria.

Within modern society, however, the individual's several affiliations are not arranged predictably and consistently with respect to one another; rather, they overlap, cut across one another, *intersect.* A different individual may occupy each point of intersection between the social circles. As a result, an individual can identify with a potentially unique packet of affiliations. This follows from the fact that the progress of modernity allows or indeed urges the individual to *choose* those affiliations as she moves from the sphere of family relations to those of religion, work, politics, leisure, and aesthetic and cultural experience. In doing so, it becomes more likely that the individual will approach and be admitted to (or undertake to build) ever new circles, each shared mostly by different associates; and that the status she holds within each circle will not be closely correlated with or predictable from that held within others. This pattern renders the dynamics of each group relatively "opaque" with respect to the others, shielding the individual from close and persistent scrutiny on the part of her associates. This engenders a sense of anonymity, which in turn may feed a sense of autonomy.

This modern phenomenon of progressive individualization is of great interest to Simmel, who, although aware of its limitations and risks, evaluates it positively. In doing so, he distances himself from an attitude toward modernity—well characterized by the expression "cultural pessimism"—widely held in the Germany of his time among intellectuals and among academics within the social and historical disciplines. Cultural pessimism emphasized and considered as negative many aspects of modernity, notably atomization, individualism, materialism, devaluation of tradition, cultural relativism, worship of science and technology, and faith in progress.

Simmel does not completely dissociate himself from some of these positions. For instance, his thesis that within modernity the progress of the "objective spirit"—that is, knowledge, organizational practices, political and economic institutions—tends to outpace that of the "subjective spirit"—the individual's ability to comprehend, assimilate, and evaluate such phenomena—may be seen as a variant of the contrast cultural pessimists posited between *Zivilisation* (bad!) and *Kultur* (good!). But to a greater extent, Simmel feels that modern society engenders increasing opportunities for manifesting and realizing intrinsic potentialities of human nature that premodern society tended to suppress or consider deviant: the individual's ability to escape the hold of preestablished, often pressing and suffocating, affiliations, and to confront critically prevailing beliefs, preferences, and norms. In summary, in Simmel's view *one* central human value—individual freedom—asserts itself within modernity, however in a partial, controversial, discontinuous, and sometimes contradictory fashion, and at some unavoidable cost to other values.

THE PHILOSOPHY OF MONEY

Simmel develops this argument in several writings, but in the most explicit and sustained manner in an entire, lengthy chapter of his *Philosophy of Money*, an exemplary sociological treatment of the phenomenon of money considered as a social institution (in the wording of some passages of the text: as an aspect of the "objective spirit," an expression derived from Hegel). That is, money is a fundamental expression—found repeatedly in history, although with quite diverse manifestations and to a varying extent—of a social group's ability to produce material and ideal objects (particularly, among the latter, systems of ideas and rules) whereby it can manage aspects of its relations with other social groups and with nature. The central sociological aspect of money is its critical role within exchange, the phenomenon from which Simmel derives all economic experience.

Once more, *ungesellige Geselligkeit* is in evidence in this emphasis on exchange. As Adam Smith points out in the opening pages of *The Wealth of Nations*, it is through exchange that various suppliers (the butcher, the brewer, the baker) make goods and services available that satisfy others' needs. In so doing, they are motivated not by benevolence toward them but rather by the intent to satisfy their own needs. In any case, exchange relations are rendered infinitely easier to establish and manage, more efficient, and more calculable in their consequences (in particular the relationship they establish, in each exchange act, between acquisition and renunciation) when they go beyond mere barter and take the form, typically, of sell-and-purchase transactions. Here, the exchange relation itself is mediated by money, that is, by an object of certain, stable, publicly declared and guaranteed value, which makes *commensurable* the moment of sale/renunciation and the moment of purchase/acquisition in the exchange itself, whatever its subjects, times, places, objects, and modalities. By this account, all economic subjects can be presumed to possess, expect, and accept money.

All of *The Philosophy of Money* discusses, besides the nature of money and its fundamental function in economic relations, the social, cultural, and political presuppositions and consequences of money's existence and of the forms it takes within various historical situations. The fourth chapter expressly and thoroughly examines the relationship between the monetary economy, in the particularly advanced and sophisticated form it takes in modern society, and the freedom of the individual.

As we observed, this freedom should not be considered a condition of total insulation and self-sufficiency on the part of the individual. Instead, it constitutes a particular configuration of social relations, which presupposes and determines for the individual a relationship with social reality that we might label "disengagement." Typically, the modern individual does not often and willingly enter into particularly absorbing and involved relations; rather, she maintains a distance from others that is both concrete and metaphorical and undertakes and manages relations with others objectively, focusing them on different, abstract aspects of reality.

Let us consider briefly how money allows, or indeed requires or at any rate facilitates, such a relationship between the individual and the surrounding social reality. First, compared to other resources such as real estate ownership or certain occupational qualifications and capacities, possession of money does not leave (as it were) a visible, enduring imprint on the individual or strictly determine his attitudes and initiatives. One might say that for the individual money produces a disengagement between what he has (*Haben*) and who he is (*Sein*); it frees its possessor from highly constraining and limiting determinations. To support this statement, Simmel mentions the protracted sequence as a result of which, in early modern Europe, landowning lords ceased to demand of their rustic dependents specific work performances or dues in kind (delivery of specific quantities of certain staples, a number of compulsory days of unpaid work) and converted them into periodic money payments. This allowed their dependents to decide for themselves what to grow or raise in their family holdings, and exchange part of it on the market for the sums the lords now expected from them as rent.

In *The Passions and the Interests* (1977), Albert Hirschman emphasizes a similar effect of the modern shift of the center of the economic system from landed to mobile wealth. A landowner is always exposed to the possibility of the sovereign expropriating him, say through banishment; this makes the land-wealthy more vulnerable and likely to yield to the sovereign's demands, however unjustified. Mobile wealth has its prototype in money and protects those possessing it from such a threat; thus its progression to the center of the economy became an aspect of modern constitutionalization of political domination and the rise of liberal regimes.

Furthermore, Simmel argues, money is an abstract object, which cannot directly satisfy concrete needs but merely renders *commensurable* the most diverse things, and allows itself to be possessed entirely and used wholly at the behest of whoever possesses it. Therefore, whether spent or held, money can be used to fully express the subject's intents, preferences, and economic interests. As Simmel explains:

It would be possible to construct a scale of objects based on the extent to which the will can take command of them . . . or the extent to which they can really be "possessed." Money would be located at the extreme end of such a scale. . . . Money lacks that structure by which other specific objects, even if we legally own them, refuse to yield to our will. . . . Money itself complies equally with every directive with regard to the object, the extent of expenditure, the speed of spending or retaining. In this manner, money grants to the self the most complete freedom to express itself in an object. . . . All that money is and has to offer is given without reservation to the human will and is completely expressed by the will [Simmel, 1978: 325].

The experience of disengagement, and thus of liberation, that money affords the individual is revealed also in the close relationship between money and the market. According to Simmel, this is a paradox in modern society:

The subjective feeling of freedom rests on the very fact that who lives in an advanced economy depends on an ever-increasing number of individuals; for these have for the subject a merely objective significance, purely qua carriers of functions, means to the satisfaction of needs; whatever else they are as persons never comes into consideration. . . . How many are the suppliers on whom he depends under a money economy! Yet he is incomparably more independent with respect to any single one of them, and he can change that one easily and at will [Simmel,1989: 721].

The larger the network of individual dependencies, the more the individual is disengaged from it with respect to each particular dependency, and the less subject to the others involved in the network. Also in this fashion, the expressly monetary nature of the modern market economy entails an affirmation of individual freedom. This of course holds if and only to the extent that a given individual possesses money. Perhaps Simmel does not take sufficiently into account a statement found in the Scriptures: *homo sine pecunia imago mortis* ("a man without money is an image of death").

Furthermore, money is *par excellence* the instrument and the measure of the individual's choices—what we might call his elective behaviors, which as we have seen play a large role also in Simmel's understanding of the modern "web of group affiliations." This is due among other things to the fact that money is easily and clearly divisible; it can be partitioned into exceedingly small quantities, each of which in being held or expended closely reflects the precise order of significance the subject assigns to its employment within the universe of his or her own needs and interests.

Further: money can represent, convey, and transmit in a compendious manner even huge amounts of economic value. This is evident if we compare the physical objects that serve as carriers of money itself with the material values to which they refer; it is especially clear if we compare paper money to coins, and even more if we compare banknotes themselves with other monetary instruments, both those known to Simmel (checks, bills of exchange, company shares) and later ones (credit cards, electronic money vehicled by computers via satellites).

This succession of ever faster and less substantial monetary vehicles reveals more openly the intrinsically *symbolic* nature of money itself. In all its forms, money intervenes in the economic process not because of its material substance, its direct bearing on needs, but thanks to its mere capacity to represent, ordain, and compare in quantitative terms an infinite variety of goods and services, allowing them to be more easily exchanged, produced, and accumulated.

To perform this function optimally, money, in whatever form, must meet two requirements. First, it must constitute a certain and stable carrier of economic value; only on this condition can it operate as the "immovable mover" of the economic process. Second, in operating this way money unavoidably depends, at every moment and in all aspects of the process, on the *trust* accorded it by all subjects, their disposition to unproblematically assume that everyone will accept money as a vehicle and measure of economic value. In other words, money always rests (to use the term in a broader meaning) on *credit*. It requires trust that the money we accept can in turn be expended at the same value. (This insight, however derived, has been lately deployed to understand and explain significant contemporary financial crises.)

Conceivably, having lived in a phase of European economic history that did not experience rapid mass inflation, Simmel was not aware of the close connection between those two requirements. He is, however, aware that they both presuppose a public, legally enforceable guarantee of the value of money, thus its "general acceptability" as a means of payment. He also saw that, under modern conditions, such a guarantee could be afforded to economic subjects only by a unified and commandeering political structure: the state.

The following brief quote from *The Philosophy of Money* is another general proposition:

Without the general trust that people have in one another, society itself would disintegrate, for very few relationships are based entirely upon what is known with certainly about another person, and very few relationships would endure if trust were not as strong as, or stronger than, rational proof or personal observation [Simmel, 1978: 178].

This sentence may remind the reader of one cited in a previous chapter, from Durkheim's *Elementary Forms of Religious Life*. Let us reconsider it: "Let the idea of society be extinguished in individual minds, let the beliefs, traditions, and aspirations of the collectivity be felt and shared by individuals no longer, and society will die."

To what extent can one reasonably view these two statements as equivalent? Some similarities are obvious, but there are also noteworthy contrasts, indicating substantially different understandings between the two theorists. (Durkheim and Simmel, in fact, were not simply contemporaries; each knew of the other's sociological writings.) First, note the linguistic difference between Durkheim's "dying" and Simmel's "disintegrating." The former suggests a conception of society as an organic being, capable of life and death. The latter suggests an image of society as a constructed reality, a structure.

There is also a significant difference between Durkheim's "collectivity" and Simmel's "men." The first notion suggests what is sometimes called a holistic conception of the intellectual object of sociology, the latter an individualistic one. In methodological terms, one might say, we are implicitly advised by Durkheim to take what is sometimes called a "katascopic" perspective (from top to bottom, from the whole to the parts) and by Simmel to take an "anascopic" one (from bottom to top, from the parts to the whole). Consistent with this, the statements suggest that the persistence of society depends on different conditions. In Durkheim, the collectivity must continue to make its own, to identify with, a unitary ensemble of ideas and norms; in Simmel, individuals must continue to establish with one another relations underwritten by their reliance on the other's conduct.

Another passage from *Philosophy of Money* clearly expresses the author's conception of society and the difference from Durkheim's.

The exchange of the products of labour, or of any other possessions, is obviously one of the purest and most primitive forms of human socialization; not in the sense that "society" already existed and then brought about acts of exchange but, on the contrary, that exchange is one of the functions that creates an inner bond between men—a society, in place of a mere collection of individuals. Society is not an absolute entity that must first exist so that all individual relations of its members . . . can develop within its framework or be represented by it: it is only the synthesis or the general term for the totality of these specific interactions [Simmel, 1978: 175].

The relationship we have called disengagement—it could also be called detachment or distance—is characteristic of the modern individual *in relation to his or her social* counterparts in social relations, or indeed vis-à-vis the relations themselves. It has a further correlation, revealing itself in the increasingly sharp contrast within modernity between the complexities of the individual's subjective experiences on the one hand and, on the other, the objectivity more clearly vested in the reality of which the subject is part but with which it also is confronted. As Simmel writes:

The intellectual world of classical antiquity differs from that of modern times chiefly in the fact that only the latter has, on the one hand, developed a comprehensive and clear concept of the Ego, as shown by the significance of the problem of liberty which was unknown in ancient times; and on the other, expressed the independence and force of the concept of the object through the idea of unalterable laws of nature [Simmel, 1978: 64].

The contrast has more than just purely intellectual aspects. In the course of modernization it also has embodied itself within concrete dimensions of daily existence.

During the last three hundred years . . . on the one hand the laws of nature, the material order of things, the objective necessity of events emerge more clearly and distinctly, while on the other we see the emphasis upon the independent individuality, upon freedom, upon independence [*Fürsichsein*, literally "being for oneself"] . . . in relation to all external and natural forces becoming more and more acute and increasingly stronger [Simmel, 1978: 302].

According to Simmel, various characteristics of modern mentality reflect the central position held in society by the economic sphere and the monetary mechanism. The most significant and pervasive characteristic is the intellectualization of the conduct of existence, which reflects (and to an extent is required by) the fact, again, that money is by nature an *instrument* of gratification, without directly gratifying qualities of its own. Furthermore, money requires of its possessor a disposition to consider and compare alternative uses of it, and to construct and manage long chains of means-and-ends relations. On this account, "the growth of intellectual abilities and of abstract thought characterizes the age in which money becomes more and more a mere symbol, neutral as regards its intrinsic value" (Simmel, 1978: 152).

Additionally, one may associate with money the modern tendency to em-phasize the quantitative aspects of reality, a disposition to calculate, to "take into account" in the original meaning of the expression. This tendency finds expression in the stress on minute and precise measurement.

The tendency to measure, weigh, calculate exactly typical of the modern era . . . seems to me causally related to the money economy, that renders necessary, in the course of daily existence, continuous mathematical operations. . . . The mathematical character of money imbues the relationship of the elements of life with a precision, a reliability in the determination of parity and disparity, an unambiguousness in agreements and arrangements in the same way as the general use of pocket watches has brought about a similar effect in daily life [Simmel, 1978: 445].

Simmel sees this stress on the quantitative confirmed by multiple aspects of modern institutions, such as conferring legitimacy on majority opinion, or the utilitarian principle of "the greatest happiness of the greatest number."

THE TRAGEDY OF CULTURE

Another feature of modernity, the accelerated pace of existence, where prompt decisions and speedy execution are frequently required, reflects money's peculiar mobility, the speed at which it can shift and transmit economic values.

Finally, the central position that economic experience and money hold within society manifests itself in modernity's materialistic and utilitarian temper. In remarking on this, Simmel introduces a critical note in his evaluation of certain social and cultural developments. For instance: "The complete heartlessness of money is reflected in our social culture, which is itself determined by money" and "Typically, money transactions engender an internal barrier between persons which the modern form of existence makes indispensable" (1978: 346).

We suggested earlier that Simmel does not share the cultural pessimism of many observers and scholars (including some sociologists) among his contemporaries. We may therefore see in these last few judgments further expression of a peculiar sensitivity for the complexities and ambivalences of all sociohistorical situations. On this account, although Simmel senses strongly that some inherent tendencies and powers of humankind find fuller and more open expression in modernity than in previous eras, there is also in his work an undertone of unease, which becomes more acute in the later writings. As modernity progresses, it becomes more likely that individuals and groups will no longer see themselves as being in control over the realities that they engender and that surround them. They may more easily lose their ability to place and keep those realities at their service.

In Hegelian and Marxist terms: in modernity, according to Simmel, the phenomenon of *alienation* becomes particularly systemic. Such unease finds clear expression in the title of an essay by the later Simmel, "The Concept and the Tragedy of Culture." But already "The Metropolis and Mental Life," an earlier and famous essay (and a ground-breaking contribution to urban sociology), without bringing into play the disquieting notion of *tragedy*, sees in the modern metropolis (which Simmel saw, admired, and loved in its most recent and conspicuous embodiment, *fin de siècle* Berlin) both a great achievement of modernity and a clear demonstration of its distinctive contradictions and dangers. Let us consider some aspects of this argument.

One can appropriately speak of a metropolis when an urban settlement becomes the privileged site of a large and growing variety of social groups, cultural forms, living practices, habitats, technological resources, and kinds of employment. Such an environment offers the inhabitants multiple and ever-changing opportunities to experience new and diverse expressions of human powers, of sociality, enjoyment, intellectual and aesthetic creativity, knowledge, taste, value, opinion. It is the ideal location *for* experimentation, for challenges to traditional, conventional, established ways of living, moving about, acquiring identities, judging oneself and one's neighbors, evaluating social trends and political authority and their initiatives, acquiring new information, forming new social movements and new collectivities. In other words, it offers the subject unparalleled occasion for appreciating the fullness of human potential, for familiarizing itself with the best legacies from the past, for becoming aware, cultivated, even sophisticated.

By the same token, however, those living in the metropolis are unavoidably at risk of finding themselves excessively stimulated and tempted, challenged by the opportunity but also perhaps overwhelmed by the obligation to keep generally informed and up-to-date, to form opinions, to deal somehow with the multitude of people surrounding them. To keep this risk at bay, they may avail themselves of resources and practices also typical of the metropolitan environment: the mass media (particularly, in Simmel's times, the daily and periodical press), mechanized means of transport that allow rapid mobility and thus easy access to various parts of the town, places (such as department stores) that assemble a great variety of commodities apt to satisfy the most diverse needs, and so forth.

Furthermore, the individual can avail herself of other distinctive aspects of urban social life. The metropolis typical hosts multiple social circles, which, as we have seen, are opaque with respect to one another and protect the individual from continuous and intrusive observation. Distinctly urban patterns of inter-individual relations allow a maximum of personal disengagement, for they are contractual in nature. They originate and can be terminated at the initiative of the individuals themselves and at their own convenience, and they refer to differentiated, changing needs and contingencies. Postures and attitudes typical of the metropolitan lifestyle allow individuals to stand aside from one another and protect their privacy in public spaces, however crowded. Also, think once more of the features associated with the great significance of money within metropolitan existence.

However, the availability of such structures and modalities of metropolitan existence may not suffice to spare individuals the experience of feeling crushed and oppressed, or at any rate overtaxed and threatened by the disproportion between the fullness of objective embodiments of technological progress, the multiple occasions of comfort, pleasure, and learning offered by the great city on the one hand; and on the other their own ability to express and satisfy demands for personal recognition, for emotional intensity in relations, for the possibility of not only gaining a superficial acquaintance with new experiences but of reflecting on them and assimilating them. The typical relations we have mentioned may allow them to feel disengaged, but they may foster attitudes of diffidence and perhaps antagonism, making it more difficult for the subject to experience trust in others and evoke their trust in return.

For these reasons, those living in the metropolis are often induced to adopt the attitude Simmel terms *blasé*. That is, they learn to underrespond to stimuli, to avoid feeling or declaring themselves particularly amused, excited, involved, instructed, and rewarded by what happens around them. However, the blasé attitude flattens and discolors, so to speak, the individual's perception of reality; it feeds in the individual a sustained indifference, even a feeling of surfeit toward the variety and changeability of metropolitan reality (the expressions "So what else is new?" and "been there, done that" characterize this attitude). In the long run, that attitude renders individuals incapable of attaching value even to their own experiences, of living them intensely and authentically.

Simmel captures this phenomenon by contrasting the *atrophy of individual culture* with the *hypertrophy of objective culture*, both typical of the metropolis. This contrast finds an echo in a broader view, variously expressed by Simmel, of modernity or indeed of social experience in general. Again, one may see in this view a variant of the thesis according to which human beings are condemned to experience alienation and find themselves in a world of which they are the authors, but which they do not perceive and experience as authors, and within which they feel lost. Finally, Simmel's analysis of money in fact confronts us with a further, unmistakable manifestation of human alienation. Money as an abstract object incapable of satisfying *immediate* concrete needs but particularly capable instead of *mediating* their satisfaction by way of expenditure makes of it, as already remarked, an intrinsically *instrumental* reality, a *means* through and through. However, on this very account money paradoxically tends to become for the individual (and particularly for the modern individual) an *end in itself*, to stoke an insatiable desire and a relentless pursuit.

REFERENCES

Hirschmann, Albert, *The Passions and the Interests*, Princeton University Press, Princeton, New Jersey, 1977.

Simmel, Georg, *The Sociology of Georg Simmel*, Free Press, Glencoe, Illinois, 1950.

Simmel, *Conflict: The Web of Group Affiliation*, Free Press, Glencoe, Illinois, 1964.

Simmel, *Philosophy of Money*, Routledge, London, 1978.

Simmel, *Philosophie des Geldes* (Georg Simmel Gesamtausgabe, band 6), Suhrkamp, Frankfurt, 1989.

5 GEORGE HERBERT MEAD

American philosopher (1863–1931). Leading figure of philosophical pragmatism and involved in several educational and urban progressive causes, spent most of his academic career at the University of Chicago researching social psychology, leaving an enduring influence on many sociology students. Mead starts from the experimental emphasis of behavioral psychology, attributing to it a peculiar "mentalist" interpretation, which will become a key element of the tradition subsequently labeled "symbolic interactionism."

SUGGESTED READINGS

Mind, Self, and Society: From the Standpoint of a Social Behaviorist, University Of Chicago Press, Chicago, 1967.
The Philosophy of the Present, Prometheus Books, Amherst, Massachusetts, 2002.
Movements of Thought in the Nineteenth Century, University of Chicago Press, 1972.

GEORGE HERBERT MEAD's inquiries originated as a sustained reflection on philosophical questions previously considered within an anthropological framework (How does self-awareness arise? How do humans differ from other animals?) or an epistemological one (What is the relation between subject and object? How is it possible to know external reality?). This reflection led Mead to adopt a fundamental viewpoint: one can confront such queries only by emphasizing the intrinsically social nature of the experiences of the "individuals" making up the human species. Mostly his beliefs elaborate this viewpoint by arguing a simple but forceful thesis: to be themselves—that is, among other things, to perceive themselves as distinct, living entities—human beings need to be thoroughly socialized. Individuals, that is, do not preexist society or enter the social process as independent, preconstituted actors. Their wishes, qualities, and features as individuals are the product of their involvement, communications, and interactions with fellow human beings. Being involved in complexes of social relations, or sharing with others ways of living, thinking, and acting, is not a threat to one's freedom but, on the contrary, a precondition to having and exercising this freedom.

THE CONSCIOUSNESS OF ONESELF

Mead begins by focusing on the nature and genesis of the consciousness of one-self. This arises in human beings from their capacity to view themselves from the outside, not just as subjects but also as the objects of their own actions. They are able to reflect on themselves and thus affect or alter what they do, and even what they want. This capacity confers on the human species a particular flex-ibility in the way it reacts to the natural environment. According to Mead, this is an evolutionary breakthrough of the same magnitude as the one that separated organisms from objects.

Actual consciousness of self, however, is a relatively rare occurrence and does not manifest itself unceasingly. When we are awake/conscious, many of the mul-tiple and diverse physiological, psychic, and social events of life take place outside of (or below) the sphere of our attention. Furthermore, Mead insists, this can be said also of some processes that in principle could activate our awareness. In fact, a significant part of human existence takes place as an unconscious flow of activities and events that do not pass the threshold of cognition we take for granted, a series of perceptions and conducts totally locked within the present, not planned and addressed to the future and not remembered. Within this flow, self-consciousness and explicit reflection intervene only insignificantly or not at all; in fact if they intervene at all they may operate as a hindrance, as when a person is engaged in a sport or a musical performance and "overthinks" it.

When and how does the consciousness of self become a phenomenon of such significance that it marks and constitutes a radically different level of human existence? As long as there is a perfect fit between the environment and us, we are not even aware of acting. We become aware when, for whatever rea-son, the flow of experience is perturbed, or the connection between our action and our environment can no longer be taken for granted. If we are submerged in water, we become aware of our own breath; a detour on the road reminds us of where we are supposed to be going; the tightness of our belt tells us that we are getting fat and makes us wonder whether we should be dieting. Such perturbations activate our mental processes. We focus our attention on the interruption of experience, we question the meaning of what we observe, we ask ourselves what sense we should attach to it. Thus, for Mead such conscious-ness or self-awareness is not a persistent property of our action but rather an aspect of the process whereby human beings notice unforeseen developments and manage the perturbations arising in their relation to the environment. Taking part in this process entails learning something about ourselves, our fellow human beings, and external nature.

What causes such perturbations in the flow of consciousness? We often say that individuals *react* to what takes place in their environment. External stimuli activate a process, which in a more or less direct manner leads to a determinate response. But Mead considers this an untenable interpretation. There *are* indeed external events, but they operate as stimuli to behavior only insofar as the organism confronting them engages in a process of perception, interpretation, and evaluation. For many animals, this process is grounded in genetically transmitted patterns of interpretation, shared by the whole species and stable over time, which make the resulting behavior highly predictable. As far as humans are concerned, this same process suggests a peculiar capacity for selecting and interpreting external events, owing to which only some are attended to and operate as stimuli to action, while others are not. Which events are selected for attention and how they are interpreted depends only to a limited extent on genetic transmission; beyond this extent it depends instead on particular schemes of interpretation and perspectives that reflect learning and are thus highly variable. Consider a case in which someone suggests that Bud Abbott has hit Lou Costello *because* Lou stepped on his foot. Such an interpretation is frequently offered, but according to Mead it is often unsatisfactory. In some situations Bud, intensely involved in other matters, might not even notice Lou's action. In others, convinced that such action was unintentional, Bud might respond amicably, and such a casual occurrence might even engender a lasting friendship. In yet other situations, Bud might keep quiet in fear of retaliation on Lou's part. In an *ancien regime* society, the actions of Bud and Lou would have been interpreted according to their respective social ranks.

When one deals with complex organisms, in other words, it is not a question of locating simple, specific relations within a given event and deriving an interpretation from them. Such organisms often interpret the same stimulus in markedly different ways. For instance, a child may be attracted by the beauty of a flame and at the same time be afraid of getting scalded. Which will prevail for a given child at a given moment: the view of the candle as something to play with, or that of the candle as a danger? Nobody can make a precise prediction, and exactly this impossibility characterizes human experience. Viewing this same situation from the child's perspective, furthermore, we realize that the contrast itself between the two aspects of the phenomenon produces a perturbation in the flow of experience. Unable simply to follow unproblematically a line of action, any action at all may be blocked by the conflict between two choices and outcomes. This perturbation has the same effects as those occurring in the external environment: the organism is induced to consider the situation as an issue, to reflect. For human beings, there is an internal environment as well as an external one.

In turn, a reflexive process, once engaged, does not produce a totally predictable outcome. According to Mead, there is no "natural" or "just" reaction to a stimulus, no *one* line of conduct every human being, if supplied with the necessary information and an adequate capacity to elaborate it, would end up choosing. That diverse interpretations may be adopted is a matter of fact; objects exist at a given time within a plurality of perspectives, each capable of imparting a meaning to the same object or event. Everything in the universe, Mead holds, can be more than one thing at once. Unlike other animal species, human beings are aware of this plurality of possibilities, which each individual experiences frequently and in diverse situations. Furthermore, the mechanisms effecting a selection from among the potential interpretive perspectives are not a direct expression of biological constitution. As a result, humans live in a world where meanings are fluid and dynamic, and where the perturbations encountered by a given line of conduct may modify not only behaviors but also the meanings attributed to them.

Humans have an extraordinary capacity for perceiving the partial nature of their own embodied perspectives, and for actively revising their own viewpoints, the meaning bestowed on objects and on their own interpretation of events. This capacity is grounded in their ability to stand back from themselves and reconsider their situation, to observe themselves as objects. Human beings can observe their own behavior as if it were another's, and ask whether a different course of action could improve on the one followed so far. Above all, they can select among the interpretations made not only of external but also of internal events, originating from within their own minds.

The mental life of humans, according to Mead, is conditioned by the outcomes of repeated experiences of this nature, the capacity to consider objectively their own perceptions, selectively focus them on diverse objects, and modify the perspective adopted toward the world. This implies that they can entertain simultaneously a plurality of perspectives and can be not only conscious (involved in a given course of action and capable, to an extent, of controlling it) but self-conscious, aware that every perspective is only one among others.

Therefore human mental life is to take part in a reflexive process entailing reference to others, reflecting a social dynamic. To reflect means to cease to identify wholly and exclusively with oneself, look at oneself from the viewpoint of another participant in the interaction, register, consider, and respond to one's own actions as if they were someone else's. Reflexivity is the interaction between a self functioning as a subject (Mead generally, but not always, calls this "the I") interested in maintaining or modifying the situation and a self reflected upon, assumed as a given (which Mead generally, but not always, calls "the Me"). It is not a matter of two differentiated "organs" within our brain or of two "characters" confronting one another in an imaginary drama. Rather, two functional dimensions of a continuous process of interpretation are involved, and management of interactions taking place within the individual's internal and external environment.

Such a dynamic of the individual's mental life has the same degree of unpredictability Mead sees in the interactions between distinct individuals. In fact, human beings are often surprised by their own actions and reactions. The stance of the actor toward his or her own objectified actions—the relation between *I* and *Me*—is to Mead no different in nature than that taking place between two interacting individuals. On the contrary, development of the individual's internal capacity for reflection depends on the ceaseless experience of social interaction with others. Only by confronting each other do human beings acquire their ability to operate simultaneously both as *I* and as *Me*.

These, therefore, are critical aspects of mental life: self-awareness, imputation of meaning to external events, and the capacity for attaching relevance to what happens, as well as for giving oneself objectives and pursuing them, and for reflecting on one's own behavior. Again, such processes are not regulated by environmental or genetic mechanisms. The organic make-up itself of the human species involves a degree of indeterminacy in the contents of the mental life of its members and a strong element of unpredictability in its concrete unfolding.

MIND, COMMUNICATION, EVOLUTION

But this does not entail that for Mead such mental life is merely idiosyncratic and locked within itself, each individual existing within a world of her own. On the contrary, his work emphasizes that individuals inhabiting a shared environment are necessarily capable of close coordination with one another. Furthermore, such coordination is required not only in order to manage the shared external environment but also to impart a degree of order to the mental life of each individual. Mead holds an even more radical view: the species and the individual, the mind and the social group, evolve together, make each other possible. It may seem as if human beings are, with respect to one another, particularly "indivisible," self-standing, and conflictual. However, the features that suggest such qualities are grounded, at base, in faculties developed within and through the social interaction of individuals. Left unable to share meanings and incapable of communicating with one another, such individuals would not be poorer or less happy; they simply would not exist.

Mead develops this view by making two distinct but convergent arguments, one relating to the forms of the inter-individual coordination characteristic of the human species and the other to the mechanisms that make such coordination between their minds possible within a highly turbulent environment. Concerning the species, he holds that their biological evolution should be viewed chiefly as social evolution; the variations in the relation between a given species and its environment cannot involve solely its individual members but can make sense only on a collective basis. For each species, there must be a strong correspondence—or at least a structural compatibility—between how individuals are organized and the forms of their social organization. If, for a given species, one considers chiefly its social structures, one may identify the kind of individual constitution they require and make possible.

Some species attain their distinctive coordination chiefly in negative terms, through repeated trial-and-error experiences. This is possible only if the constitution of the members of the species is highly flexible and relatively undifferentiated, and their reproductive processes can sustain an extremely accelerated rhythm in generating new members. Other animal species, such as insects, attain very sophisticated forms of organization entailing cooperation between distinct and highly complementary capacities, grounded in extensive organic differentiation between diverse categories of its individual members, tightly controlled in their reproduction. Thus it is with ants, and their division into various kinds of sterile wingless females, male drones, and fertile queens. Still other species rely on the uniform genetic programming of their coordination, so that any member interprets the environmental stimuli pretty much in the same way as any other. An organization of this kind requires and allows advanced development of sensorial capacities and of ways of handling the information they encounter, which come to resemble reflection. How they communicate, though, does not allow them to engage in properly reflexive processes, because animals cannot form and communicate symbols and their exchanges remain tightly programmed in genetic terms. For an example of this latter condition, Mead has his reader consider how mammals communicate. They can carry out communication he characterizes as "conversations of gestures," which can amount to an extensive, complex, and prolonged sequence of communicative acts, as in the case of two or more animals challenging one another over access to and control of resources. However, a genetic mechanism regulates such sequences; each participant reacts to the other's immediately preceding gesture but does not operate on the basis of a forecast of the one that will follow. Here, the participants are not aware of the correspondence between gesture and reaction, and each remains unable to modify its own behavior in anticipation of the behavior of the other.

When it comes to humans, however, the forms of social organization characteristic of the species are grounded almost exclusively in their communicative faculties and practices, their ability to apprehend and share one another's meanings, and the capacity to take different roles within the same interaction as well as within diverse sequences of interaction. The distinctively human form of organization is possible only because humans have a highly sophisticated sensory apparatus, a nervous system developed to the extent that it yields an extensive capacity to register, select, and symbolically interpret the events in the environment. Such capacity, furthermore, must be shared by all participants in an interaction and presupposes great similarity between individuals in terms of their organic faculties. Among humans, coordination of inter-individual activities is largely based on communication. The capacity for reflection allows human beings to become aware that for any gesture, meaning—the reactions it evokes in the participants in the interaction—can differ from what is attributed to it by whoever makes the gesture. Being aware of this difference opens up the potential inherent in the fact that a given question can have more than one meaning. When human individuals interact, the sequence of gestures may not be so much a chain of gestures and gesture reactions as anticipations of successive gestures, or the intent to evoke *certain* gestures in response.

Of course, such symbolic capacity did not appear out of the blue; it was the result of gradual and cumulative evolutionary processes, the last phases of which included development of primates' distinctive social behavior, which encompasses highly elaborate forms of inter-individual interaction. On top of this, the human species has inherited a number of capacities—language, improvisational production of tools, development of traditions, and the capacity to become aware of the partial nature of a single viewpoint or interpretation—development that can take place only in the context of collective experience. The high level of reciprocal dependency among individual members has made possible symbolic mediation, allowing humans to gain autonomy from the external and internal environments. Mead conveys this by insisting that each individual can be such only by means of membership in a community.

It is not only at the level of the species and thus in the context of extremely protracted developments that Mead argues for the joint evolution of individual and collective capacities, of individual reflexivity and social communication. This is also his thesis at the level of inter-individual interaction in historical time, where he looks for the mechanisms that make possible coordination of a multitude of individuals and continuous emergence and modification of shared meanings. How can individuals who are different from and strangers to one another come to share certain ways of feeling, acting, and thinking—to use again an expression from our discussion of Durkheim—sometimes without becoming aware of it? What mechanisms allow individuals, each of whom interprets circumstances in his own way, to end up doing so in light of common and complementary perspectives? How can individuals, each with her own history and biography, live in a world of shared meanings? In answering these queries Mead cannot but refer to the capacity of humans to distance themselves from the flow of their own experience and observe their own action as if they were *other* than themselves. Such capacity for detachment entails also a general ability to *take another's perspective*, to put oneself in the shoes of others involved in the same interaction. Such capacity lies at the very heart of reflexive processes, allowing individuals to grasp the meaning that others attach to their own actions, and to view them from the vantage point of the subjects with whom they interact. By the same token, it also lies at the heart of social interaction, allowing the individual to predict how others will react to numerous courses of action and the interaction to orient itself to a future at least partly open and contingent. It performs a fundamental role in social learning, making it possible for individuals to learn how to characterize one another's conduct, and to import into their own mental life the patterns and competences encountered in the course of interaction. By way of the individual's experience of adopting an alternative viewpoint, the models of conduct of a given society penetrate their mental processes.

Let us consider this passage more closely. For Mead, the ability to observe oneself from the viewpoint of others entails a certain degree of functional correspondence between objectified observation of oneself and objectified observation of other participants in interaction. In this sense, the dynamic taking place between *I* and *me* resembles the social interaction between two or more participants.

When something perturbs the flow of experience, this activates reflexive processes that refer to a complex of experiences, not only those of the actor itself but also how others react both to the actor's previous conduct and to actions similar to those bearing on the current problem.

Recollection of responses—rage, disgust, tolerance, understanding, approval, etc.—does not always differentiate between one's own particular responses and those of other relevant actors or spectators. According to Mead, the resulting dynamic tends to favor shared attitudes and evaluations rather than those peculiar to oneself. Whenever our own reflexive reactions replicate those socially more common, they tend to be reinforced by the great number of recollections they evoke. Correspondingly, if the former reactions differ markedly from the latter, they are less likely to be expressed and taken for granted.

Another reason for this is a tendency toward *generalization*, which Mead sees as intrinsic to the phenomenon of communication. Human beings tend to imagine spontaneously how others will interpret and account for their actions, and this applies not just to the particular others with whom they concretely interact but also to collective figures (What will *people* think? Will *the guys* like this dress?) and to abstract figures (religious entities, the ancestors, the working class, and so on). In other words, what takes place within individuals is a continuous conversation evoking and involving diverse viewpoints, whereby some interlocutors intervene more often than others or express views bearing on a greater range of themes. Some interlocutors acquire a certain influence (sometimes a particularly significant one) and push the debate, and the interpretations it evokes, in one direction or the other. Mead calls these complex, repeated, influential presences in the conversation in question *institutions*. In his view, they both structure society and at the same time shape and orient the participants' selves. Such generalized interlocutors represent the most significant mechanism for controlling individual behavior. The interventions constantly evoke within their internal debate the point of view of the collectivity—better, the collectiv*ities*—of which the individual is part. By appealing to them, the individual can anticipate how the collectivity in question will assess her own behavior, and in particular how the individual herself would assess such behavior if it were someone else's.

The development and the presence of institutions explain to some extent how human beings can attain a high degree of coordination even in turbulent and disparate environments. Such coordination, however, can also be attained thanks to a flux of communications not always appealing to a central, superior authority and its mandatory interpretation of reality. In fact, it is the operation of such a flux that permits the institutions themselves to emerge.

This operation in turn requires the availability of competent, socialized individuals drawing on a rich, shared symbolic patrimony. How are such competencies acquired? By means of what mechanisms does one attain the required capacity to observe the world from the viewpoint of another? If such a capacity is not programmed genetically in the newborn, how do we learn to coordinate ourselves with others?

MORALITY AND COMMUNICATION

Here Mead recalls his own distinction between the conversation of gestures characteristic of animals and the communication of humans. Much of what goes on with infants is a conversation of gestures, but they function chiefly as the point of departure for the learning process. Human beings can be very selective in dealing with the features and events of their environment. The newborn child gets involved in sequences of gestural conversation, but it is led to reflect on both the meaning of previous gestures and the possible consequences of responding in one manner as opposed to another. In other words, the linking of gestures reveals a correlation of the interdependence of the gestures. As growth advances, one moves on to more complex forms of gestural interaction, connecting one's own gestures to others' reactions. To do this, the child must learn to respond to his own gestures, connect his own behavior to recollection of how others reacted to similar behavior. At the next stage he will be able to predict how others will react to novel behavior, insofar as he can, however roughly, adopt the others' perspective.

As he does this, the child becomes increasingly aware of the extent to which interaction refers to generalized symbols. At first, he exists largely within a world of his own, where he reacts instinctively to concrete persons and situations, where any variation in the relation among person, situation, and gesture amounts to something of a trauma. As the process advances, the child learns to acquire greater control over how he expresses himself, as well as to interpret gestures originating from different people as amounting to the same gesture. At this point, some gestures come to be made deliberately with the intent of communicating, and the child progressively learns that a given gesture evokes similar reactions from various participants. More and more, gestures come to be employed as symbols, as something that represents something else by association, resemblance, or convention. For humans, the gestural repertory also includes language, so in the course of the child's growth it becomes increasingly possible (and necessary) to master symbolic communication, distinguish the meaning of gestures from their use in specific contexts, and put them to use in a wider range of circumstances. This engenders in the child a growing capacity for reflection and more awareness of self.

These processes require lengthy experimentation, within which there is a central role for ludic (play) behavior. It is in this context that Mead locates the chief processes whereby the newborn is transformed into a competent member of the community.

During a first, protracted phase, the child plays by impersonating concrete individuals within their own environment, including herself among the objects on which such persons act. By impersonating and entering into relations with them, the child experiments with a range of responses and reactions to her own actions. What Mead terms *play*, playful exploration, characterizes the transition from preordained sequences in the conversation of gestures to the beginning of a capacity to assume, within the interaction, the perspective of another participant. This play remains largely individual; what we see in sequence is a mere succession of roles—all played by the same child—that can easily be discontinued. Even such explorations, however, entail for the child an early process of symbolic generalization, since the reactions of diverse figures are viewed as similar.

As the child continues to grow, she adds to playful exploration a new form of play, structured by the reference to shared rules that Mead terms *game*. Here it is not sufficient for the child to identify with a concrete person; identification is now required with one role among others. Each role, furthermore, has meaning and sense only within an entire complex of roles, each referring to specific rules and objectives that such rules posit. Said otherwise, participating in a proper game requires participants to have the capacity to view themselves from several viewpoints. The roles themselves are not identical with concrete persons but with positions in the game, which in some cases refer to a single player or role (a goalkeeper, a catcher) but in others to collective entities (the team). Furthermore, in such circumstances playing does not require simply being aware of others' viewpoints but also allowing such viewpoints to influence one's own, even if this requires giving priority to an external interest instead of to one's own.

Although within playful exploration the child learns to take the point of view of other individuals, in the context of the game she becomes able to take the positions of those Mead calls *generalized others*, abstract members of units representing participants in every individual's internal dialogue. Finally, Mead characterizes two significant classes of generalized others: those standing for concrete social groups, with which the participant identifies as a member with direct experience in this kind of social relation; and functionally defined groups, such as those indebted to banks or lovers of western films—that is, particularly broad and inclusive internal interlocutors.

Therefore, in the process of being socialized the newborn undergoes various phases, each with its own level of complexity in the relations and the symbols it comprises. Starting from prevalently gestural conversations, the child, as his capacity to take on the viewpoints of other figures in the interactions grows, develops his own capacity for both symbolic mediation and anticipating future interactional events. As he engages in more structured interaction forms involving greater numbers of interacting figures, the child learns to assume the point of view of collective and abstract units, at first organized (the cricket team), and subsequently functional in nature (teamwork!).

As this process unfolds, the child's reflexive capacity grows to the point where she can evaluate comparatively the significance of alternative courses of action with reference to what she can expect in response to each. Once she has fully developed such capacity—allowing her at least to some extent to act while seeing herself as if from outside, imagining how others may interpret and judge her own action—the child has become a competent member of society. The external import of such capacity is that the "newcomer's" reactions to her own actions will have progressively aligned themselves to those they would evoke in the other participants.

One may raise objections to some of Mead's arguments. The notion that the mechanisms of social coordination systematically privilege the viewpoint most widely shared within the community may seem to emphasize and encourage the subject's capacity to conform. The strong role attributed to the generalized other may be viewed as conferring greater moral significance to the ends of groups and organizations, against those of the individuals who make them up. Such objections are largely unwarranted. It is indeed the case that Mead seeks chiefly to capture how a social group's models intervene on an individual's mental processes. It is also true that for Mead the individual's disposition to adhere, within his own internal dialogue, to the most widely sounded voice, that of the whole community, constitutes a higher form both of morality and of rationality.

It is important, however, that such positions be understood with reference to the theoretical perspective within which they were articulated. In the first place, Mead considers that humans live in a highly turbulent environment. Their habits and traditions are constantly challenged by various sorts of disruptions and inconsistencies, many of which originate from the reflexive processes of individuals, from experiences taking place within local chains of interaction. If it is the case that actors often perceive reality through inadequate or unjust perspectives, including some of a moral nature, such conventional morality is repeatedly put in doubt by new problems, actors, and interpretive perspectives. Mead adds to this that such perturbations activate reflexive processes also in the social field. They cause the framing of new issues, and open up the possibility of new values to attain a voice, for new actors to assist in formulating more abstract and inclusive moral criteria.

Through this endless process of moral re-articulation, the presence of generalized others in internal conversation plays a twofold role. Directly, it opens up a critical perspective on the existing social order, because there is always some discrepancy between it and the principles by which it professes to be inspired; such normative reference makes it possible to articulate with respect to a given community a critical discourse not utterly alien to it. To be heard, such a critique must be able to enter and participate in the entirely internal conversation. Indirectly, the presence of generalized interlocutors in the dialogue internal to individuals makes possible a process of generalization surpassing the boundaries of the social units. According to Mead, in fact, communication engenders solidarity, which does not stop at such boundaries but tends to shift them and include ever new potential interlocutors in the circuit of communication. This applies also to generalization processes; the more inclusive generalized other comes to include the whole ensemble of potential participants in communication. In this manner, the presence of generalized others suggests a constant tendency to broaden, rather than narrow, the boundaries of communication, and thus of solidarity. By emphasizing the role that shared normative frameworks play in shaping individuals as they appear in history, Mead expresses his conviction that discourses can come to be shared only to the extent that they expose themselves to continuous revision and change.

6 TALCOTT PARSONS

American sociologist (1902–1979). After having studied in England and Germany, he taught for his entire career at Harvard University, where he was among the founders of the Department of Social Relations. His main effort was development of "action theory," intended as a shared analytical framework for the social sciences, able to highlight the specifically sociological component of the framework. This theoretical effort, although sometimes expounded in frequently opaque language, received great attention and evoked much controversy, conferring to Parsons, for a while, a central and commanding position within the discipline at the international level.

SUGGESTED READINGS
The Structure of Social Action, Free Press, New York, 1967.
The Social System, Free Press, 1991.
Toward a General Theory of Action (with Edward Shils), Transaction, New Brunswick, New Jersey, 2001.
Politics and Social Structure, Free Press, 1969.
American Society, Paradigm, Boulder, Colorado, 2007.

FOR ITS COMPLEXITY AND DIVERSITY, all of Parsons's sociological thinking presupposes a particular view of human action, variously elaborated in his writings, which we may call a *normative* view. Here, all human action is seen as an effort to manage and modify the gap between the world as it presents itself to the actor (the *situation*) and what according to the actor the world *ought* to be like. Every action, no matter how banal or insignificant, constitutes an attempt to modify the situation and render it more similar to what the actor thinks it should be. This attempt to align the real to the normative engenders continuous tension. On the one hand, what the actor would like to do is always at variance with what the constraints (*conditions*) of the situation and the available *means* allow him or induce him to do; not all that the actor wishes were the case is in fact feasible. Furthermore, there are always more aspects to the ideal state of things than one has energy, time, and disposition to bring about at a given moment.

All of us, and always, would like very often to be somewhat richer than we are, devote more attention to our dear ones, drink another beer with our buddies, be a better citizen, improve our spiritual well-being, and so on.

Therefore every actor must endlessly choose, establish priorities, and privilege certain aspects of his or her condition at the expense of others. This entails that all attempts to align more perfectly the actual situation and the normative model require of the actor an *effort*, expending energy and emotion, juggling contrasting pressures, pursuing desired ends by employing available means.

On the other hand, according to Parsons, human beings do not constitutionally possess a clear understanding of an ideal condition from which to derive the preferences and the normative objectives actors *ought* to seek and pursue. To the contrary, actors will view and assess a situation in radically different ways, seek to bend it in the direction of diverse and often contrasting targets, and develop incomparable and sometimes idiosyncratic preferences. In sum, all actors operate in a context characterized by both conditional and normative elements, but their action never follows automatically from them. Except in extreme instances, the choice of means is not directly imposed by the shape of the situation; nor is the choice of objectives directly imposed by the normative components. Even whether or not action itself takes place does not depend exclusively on external conditions, but also on an intrinsically contingent internal element such as individual effort.

THE PROBLEM OF THE SOCIAL ORDER

For Parsons, the key problem is to explain how, in light of this irreducible autonomy of the actors, a *social order* can emerge and operate that allows their reciprocal actions to be relatively foreseeable and coordinated. Acknowledging the complexity of the subjective determinants of action and the autonomy of the actors means, in fact, to assume that the relations between any two actors are at base *un*predictable and indeed loaded with potential conflict. In fact, each actor's autonomy induces in those dealing with him a degree of uncertainty as to how he will conduct himself toward them. Consequently, if one seeks to account for social life by appealing to individual behavior as the sole explanatory criterion (an approach Parsons terms *atomism*), one unavoidably ends up viewing it as a mire of unpredictable and conflictual interactions. As a result, from an atomistic perspective one cannot account for the fact that every day we experience the social world as operating in a (relatively) orderly and predictable fashion, where mutually independent actors manage to understand one another and coordinate their respective activities.

According to Parsons, if social theory is to account for the autonomy and independence of actors, by the same token it must explain the operations of those mechanisms of institutional regulation that, in spite of their autonomy and independence, make it possible for actors to interact in a relatively orderly and predictable fashion. To attain this, however, individualistic atomism must yield to a more complex view, within which such autonomy and independence are not taken as facts of nature but appear to result from a complex process of growth, wherein the individual's biological and psychological dimensions continuously interact with the social and cultural dimensions (*institutionalized individualism*).

Difficult as it may be to do, such a view must be spelled out theoretically. Otherwise, Parsons insists, students will find themselves always compelled to stress exclusively *either* the actor's autonomy, and leave indeterminate the description of the social world, *or* the social order, and surrender this autonomy completely to the deterministic operation of genetic or environmental constraints. What one needs, instead, is to explain coherently that one theory can have *both* independent actors *and* institutions regulating their interactions. How is one to do this?

Parsons's argument becomes even more complex. He states that the mechanisms of social coordination cannot be grounded in, and supported by, self-conscious acceptance by actors of rules, as if they freely subscribed to a social contract. A highly autonomous actor, exclusively motivated by the intent of attaining her goals, would soon enough discover that on many occasions the best way to do so lies in violating those rules instead of abiding by them. Why should this actor not act as a lion or a fox—that is, resort to violence and fraud, if doing so were the most efficient way to get what she wants? And why should other actors, anticipating such a possibility, not conclude that it is in their interest to beat her to it? These queries suggest that the social order cannot be grounded in a set of rational rules of conduct, explicitly agreed to by the actors. It ought to be considered, instead, as an unforeseen consequence of human action, a set of mechanisms that actors constantly generate and support, but do so indirectly. Such mechanisms, according to Parsons, derive from the peculiar role performed by normative elements, by conceptions of what is desirable (even if it does not happen to be desired by a given actor).

Parsons contends that as actors enter any social interaction they encounter the problem he sometimes labels "double contingency." That is, every actor must anticipate the goals and preferences of others and understand whether and how to coordinate his own conduct with theirs. On the other hand, however, every actor must take into account that those actors with whom he seeks to interact are themselves oriented by *their own* interpretations of *his own* acts. Whoever seeks to interpret the preferences of other actors is the object of interpretation; whoever seeks to make the actions of the other the means to his own goals is a potential means for the goals of others; whoever attaches value to the reactions of others is a potential text for recognition; and whoever judges can be judged.

This is a peculiarity of relations among human actors. When we pick a tool out of a toolbox, our criterion for judgment is merely to determine whether or not it is suitable for sinking a nail into a plank. We need not wonder what the hammer thinks of our action. The problem changes, though, when we deal with other (equally self-willed) actors. To choose what is best for us to do, we must anticipate what those other actors will make of our activities, how they will react to the choices open to us, to be able to select the alternative most likely to induce them to react as we wish. If I behave in a friendly manner, will I be considered an amiable person with whom one can do business, or as an overeager fool? If I make a high bid, will it get me what I want, or encourage even higher bids from others? If I boast to Tom about something that in fact has been done by Dick, will Tom get on the phone to Dick and reveal my lie? If, instead of the customary bunch of flowers, I offer my hosts a basket of tasty vegetables, will this be viewed as something nice, or as the gesture of someone who will do anything to make an impression?

From a purely rational perspective, social interaction would require each actor to anticipate all possible courses of action open to all the other interacting individuals, and compare their outcomes to decide which best suits her own goals. Parsons holds that such a procedure would quickly exhaust the human brain's capacity for calculation. Even simple social interactions, in fact, are fairly complicated. One must thus acknowledge, Parsons argues, that if independent actors are to assume a certain level of predictability in social actions and thus make sensible choices, some *meta*-individual mechanisms must intervene in the process. These mechanisms would establish, and to some degree impose priorities among, the possible alternatives, thereby reducing for each participant in the interaction the range of possible reactions from the others. According to Parsons, such a role can be performed, within social interaction, only by a *shared normative order*, rooted in a common culture and supported by a system of sanctions, positive or negative, known to the greater part of the participants.

We may ask at this point why Parsons stresses that such shared culture should be normative in nature. One can easily imagine even fairly complex social interactions where the sustained mutual acquaintance of the participants, generated over the course of many previous occasions, permits easy prediction of each other's behavior. Does one not say, indeed, that the soundest friendships are those where the friends no longer need to talk to one another? There are many situations where it is not particularly problematic to anticipate even the goals of totally unknown actors. If someone, from a low-flying airplane, begins to drop thousands of hundred-dollar bills onto the streets, it is not difficult to foresee what will be done by the passersby. Finally, in many situations there is such a discrepancy between the resources available to one actor or group and those available to others that the former need not bother predicting the reactions of the latter.

Parsons does not deny the possibility and the empirical relevance of such nonnormative aspects of the relationship between actors. He does hold that such aspects (he labels them *factual*) can occur and operate only locally, and even then only with considerable difficulty. Once more, the reason for this lies in the actor's autonomy, as a consequence of which nothing in an actor's past can guarantee he will behave in a precisely predictable manner in the future. Sometimes it is the most committed and scrupulous employee who at a certain point makes off with the contents of the firm's safe, and sometimes a stone tossed aside by the builders becomes a cornerstone. Any interaction is thus perpetually subject to unexpected developments and to the disappointment of expectations that in the past structured it. If all actors constantly had to monitor the flow of the interaction in order to align their expectations to ongoing reality, the cognitive effort needed to sustain the interaction would become unbearable. Every disappointment of expectations would be ascribed to the expectant actor himself, who has shown his naiveté.

If social life operated on such premises, Parsons contends, actors would find it reasonable to interact as little as possible with others, and distance themselves from it at the least chance of personal failure. This is not the way things function in reality. According to Parsons, in the critical moments of the interactive process actors do not attend to the regularities of one another's behavior; rather, they comport themselves on the basis of "how such things ought to be done." In other words, normative expectations make social interaction orderly. Actors consider themselves bound to respect and enact those expectations, even if unaware that by doing so they expose themselves to some amount of risk and uncertainty. Given this, if other actors' conduct appears to vary from what is expected and the expectation is normatively (socially) sanctioned, an actor will not impute such variance to his or her own naiveté but to those who violated the expectation, thus confirming (at any rate in the near future) the normative definition of the situation.

Parsons holds that the normative ordering of interaction requires participants to share generalized preferences (values) defining the situation, as well as more specific expectations concerning the conduct of given individuals or roles (norms). The first component is a definition of reality, which is assumed, taken for granted by all actors no matter how much they differ from one another. In other words, what we find here are definitions of the *desirable*, not necessarily what is actually *desired*—broad descriptions of what may be legitimately imputed to be an acknowledged priority all actors hold in this situation. That is, sharing values allows all the actors to assume they know what other participants want or desire. The second component is constituted by more elaborate and differentiated sets of expectations that strongly curb the unpredictability of individual behavior by referring to a model of conduct that, should it be questioned, could be seen to reflect the more general definitions of the situation. I expect the letter carrier to deliver my correspondence, a barista to prepare and hand me a cup of coffee in exchange for a certain sum of money, my spouse to treat me in a familiar way. The existence of shared norms thus allows interaction participants to guess how other partners will react to their own actions. Together these components, being shared by the actors, strongly reduce the complexity and contingency of interaction by bringing into being an environment allowing a substantial level of reciprocal predictability. This predictability can be maintained and reproduced insofar as the shared normative elements, should some expectations be dropped, justify application of sanctions against the responsible parties.

So far, then, Parsons has argued for the necessity of a shared system of normative expectations *if* social interaction is to proceed in a relatively orderly fashion. But how can such a system maintain and reproduce itself by resisting the erosion and threat of unsustainability entailed in the passage of time? To address this question, Parsons turns his attention to the social processes that allow (or do *not* allow) the actors' motivational energies to mix with cultural components such as shared values and norms, with social structures (in particular the fact that actors generally have unequal access to resources, and thus differing capacities for bringing to bear positive or negative sanctions).

The most important such processes, according to Parsons, are of two kinds: those of *socialization*, whereby cultural models are selectively incorporated into the actors' psychological structures; and those of *institutionalization*, whereby those same cultural models are instead selectively incorporated into the system of social rewards. For the social order to be stable, these two kinds of processes must be coordinated and mutually reinforcing. On this account, Parsons considers social interaction the integrative component of action, the process whereby the socialized needs and wants of actors become compatible with the normative and factual schemes of the situation within which individuals interact.

Sociological analysis can thus be anchored to an ideal condition that Parsons calls *perfect institutional integration of individual motivations*, in which those processes are not only individually effective but also perfectly compatible and interwoven. Here, actors direct themselves toward socially desirable goals and seek to realize them by employing means that are socially legitimate (or even favored or expressly enjoined). In doing so, they initiate social interactions by which their actions are positively evaluated by the other participants, which leads to satisfactory outcomes rewarding that way of behaving. In this hypothetical situation, in other words, all social processes mutually sustain and reinforce one another, and the actors' expectations complement each other and jointly affirm their common reference to the normative order.

Parsons has often stressed that this ideal picture is an abstract, theoretical point of reference, not a description of actual circumstances. In his view, this approximates, within sociological theory, the role played in economic theory by the concept of a perfectly competitive market, and it shares comparable remoteness from empirical reality. The advantage of such a sociological ideal model, according to Parsons, is that it can be purposefully compared to a range of empirical situations, establishing in what way and to what extent each locates itself at some distance from the model. From this perspective, paying attention to those varying distances, it becomes possible to study systematically the mechanisms of social control. These are the social activities confronting the unavoidably limited and imperfect manner in which institutional integration exists and operates, so that such integration cannot be rejected and replaced by forms of integration exclusively factual rather than normative in nature.

As a result, processes of socialization and institutionalization are required for the existence of a structured system of social interactions (the *social system*); they set the degree and nature of a normative order that ordains and stabilizes interaction and affords actors the motivational and psychological energies needed to undertake and manage their activities. In other words, those processes unite the social dimension of human conduct and its psychological and cultural dimensions. The same processes, though, do not determine the course of social interaction; they make its regulation possible but do not establish effective operation. If we are to see precisely how cultural, psychological, and social factors interact, we need to undertake a specific analysis of the social dimension.

This entails, in the first place, understanding how it is possible not just to manage an interaction but to coordinate a huge number of social interactions developing alongside one another, and yet display innumerable, significant, direct and indirect, positive and negative relations with one another.

THE SOCIAL SYSTEM

This structural interdependence is particularly complex and problematical because it exerts pressure in many directions and requires constant adjustment. How can one study such a variety of mutual tensions and adaptations, which is apparently infinite and changes all the time? Parsons holds that the coordination problems confronting any social system—from a couple to world society—can be subsumed under a relatively small number of significant, recurrent problems. Once they are identified, it is possible to analyze systematically and comparatively the process of institutional regulation of social interactions.

At first, Parsons thought there were just two such processes. On the one hand, any social system must regulate the distribution of resources among participants (*allocation*); on the other, it must make sure that the various institutional complexes are compatible with one another (*integration*). This last problem also concerned compatibility between normative models, mechanisms of social control, and procedures for settlement of disputes. During the 1950s, however, he put forward and elaborated *AGIL*, a fourfold set of fundamental problems confronting all social systems.

First, each social system must deal with the problem of how to acquire and mobilize resources drawn from the natural environment, thereby attaining a stable relationship with its nonsocial context (*adaptation*). The second problem lies in establishing equilibrium between the shared goals of the system as a whole and those of each unit within, and in deciding when and how the former are entitled to priority over the latter (*goal attainment*). Third, each social system must adopt mechanisms for managing the relations between the system's units, defining the relative memberships, handling conflict, and settling disputes (*integration*). The fourth and final problem is how to ensure that individuals will form and observe commitments to the system, its identity, and its shared values; and how to elaborate and affirm its cultural models, countering phenomena that might make them appear less cogent and significant (*latent pattern maintenance*).

To Parsons, no social system can disregard any of these four requirements, none of which can be subsumed by another. One cannot say that pursuit of collective goals is always more urgent than maintenance of latent models, or suggest that at base the adaptation function ranks above integration. Consequently, every social system must deal with all four problems at the same time, without definitively solving any of them. By this account, it is always necessary to accept and manage a certain level of tension among the four problems and among their respective solutions—and this imparts to social systems an inherent unsettled dynamic. Even in analyzing social systems, then, we encounter the tension between the existing and the possible, the conditional and the normative, which—as we have argued—Parsons stressed from the beginning in his analysis of individual action.

One can better understand to what uses Parsons seeks to put this conceptual scheme by seeing how he employs it in analyzing specific social systems. He has done so with varying plausibility, sometimes straining a bit too hard to constrain the realities in question within his fourfold scheme. A good example is his analysis of *modern societies*. In his writings, this expression basically designates (not without frequent ambiguity) nation-states of considerable dimensions, capable of maintaining a certain degree of self-sufficiency with respect to their environment (including fellow comparable units of the same scale) and internally articulated into institutional complexes that are highly differentiated from one another and distinctively structured. In such contexts, Parsons associates (1) the society's *adaptive* function with its economic system, which turns nonsocial resources into goods and services to be consumed in society; (2) the society's *goal-attainment* function with its political system, which establishes the proper relations between the "private" goals of single units (individuals and groups) and those considered instead to be collective and binding; (3) the *integrative* function with the *societal community*, that is, the complexes of activities (including those of a juridical nature) that commit citizens to various forms of solidarity and determine for each one the rights he or she is to enjoy; and (4) the function of *pattern maintenance* with those Parsons terms fiduciary institutions, thus those of the family, religion, art, and education, which ensure that cultural models will remain significant and be transmitted from one generation to the next.

Parsons stresses that this correspondence between functional problems and specific organizational and structural forms must be handled with care. In the first place, one and the same structure can perform different functions in different times and places. For instance, the family has been for centuries (and to an extent still is) a critical institution also for the adaptive sphere of production.

As a result, one can associate certain subsystems of society with given institutional complexes only in functional terms, attending to the nonintentional consequences of the workings of those complexes and not just to the meanings expressly envisaged by the participants. In the second place, every collectivity is itself a system and must manage all four functional problems. Even a monastery most intensely committed to spiritual concerns must secure a minimum of access to economic resources. Even a firm most oriented to market processes needs to generate a sense of collective identity among its members and possess an internal hierarchy charged with setting priorities between the interests of various internal component units and between all of these and the interests of the firm as a whole. Furthermore, Parsons stresses that each subsystem of modern society—the economy, the polity, the societal community, and the fiduciary institutions—needs the others' functional performance for its own operation.

On the one hand, Parsons holds that each subsystem orients operations to values and priorities peculiar to it. In the case of the economic system, for example, the primary reference is to *utility*, in the political system to *effectiveness*, in the integrative system to *solidarity*, and in the fiduciary system to *moral integrity*. On the other hand, each of these evaluation criteria can exercise priority only if the system can attain and process resources originating from the others. It could not produce them by appealing exclusively to its own standard of operation. For example, the modern economic system can operate only within a framework where political decisions are made; conflict can be effectively regulated, moderated, and settled; contractual commitments, if necessary, can be authoritatively enforced; and the labor market can count on individuals to enter with more or less a common understanding of employment relations. All these resources are necessary to the functioning of an economic system oriented to the pursuit of profit and could not be made available if profit were the *only* criterion operative for the whole society. In the same manner, the fiduciary institutions of modern society can operate only if economic resources are abundantly produced, if political arrangements allow them the freedom to pursue their distinctive values, and if there are various forms of solidarity. None of these conditions would be satisfied if the only criterion for the distribution of social resources were the degree of attachment to given cultural or religious values.

Put otherwise, a subsystem is focused on a particular criterion but assumes implicitly the availability of social resources produced by following other criteria. According to Parsons, a high degree of interdependence between social structures and institutions practicing such different logics characterizes modern societies. Any system failing markedly in managing one of those problems is condemned to fall apart, or at least lose some of its ability to regulate the activities of the component parts. A society unable to produce economic resources to the extent required by its subsystems cannot (1) guarantee a level of individual motivation and of normative commitment capable of sustaining the complex interactions required by the other subsystems, (2) adopt sufficiently reliable procedures for coordinating activities oriented to common goals, or (3) deliver adequate integrative performances. Parsons holds that such a society would be forced to surrender independence vis-à-vis other societies and its nonsocial environment.

Note, however, that Parsons does not relate this danger exclusively to the inadequate extent to which given institutions perform their functions. It may be equally damaging if there is not sufficient integration between the circuits connecting the various subsystems. This phenomenon may be imputed in the first instance to the inadequacies of the integrative subsystem, in case it cannot keep under control—through law, but not exclusively through law—the tendency of the various subsystems each to consider its own value criterion as absolutely paramount, which Parsons calls *fundamentalism*. In fact, by assigning to all others a largely subordinate and constrained position, any "fundamentalist" subsystem runs the risk, in the long run, of sawing away the trunk of the tree on which it perches. One reason for Parsons's emphasis on systematic sociological theory is the conviction that this theory is necessary if such a problem is to be managed, by revealing that modern social structures are intrinsically pluralistic and multifunctional, and thus showing up the limitations of fundamentalist prescriptions of whatever nature (More market! More state! More solidarity! More values!).

How can one synthesize such analysis of social systems, highly abstract and focused on functional imperatives, with analysis of individual action and of previously considered social interaction? How can a multitude of actors involved in myriad practical interactions yield, even indirectly, adequate responses to the demands of the social system (adapt to the environment, attain goals, manage internal tensions, and reproduce its own normative patterns)? How can the strains suggested by the conceptual schemes, from the actor's viewpoint, come to constitute for them constraints and opportunities bearing upon attaining their own local objectives?

At a fairly late point in his intellectual career, Parsons confronted such questions by analyzing how an independent actor, interacting with other equally independent actors, may induce those partners to modify their conduct in a direction the former actor would have them follow and they would not follow without his intervention. In conceptualizing the means available to each actor seeking to obtain something from social interaction, Parsons emphasized two aspects:

The *positive* or *negative* nature of the sanction he can bring to bear in order to get others to do what he desires

The *channels* the actor can use to this end, that is, the other actors' *situation* (or circumstances) or their *intentions*

If we "cross" these two alternatives, we obtain four irreducible types of means: to provide incentives, exercise coercion, persuade, and appeal to values that an actor shares with others. Table 6.1 visualizes this conceptual operation.

	Channel	
	Situational	Intentional
Sanction		
Positive	Incentive	Persuasion
	(Money)	(Influence)
	The economy	The societal community
Negative	Coercion	Activation of value commitments
	(Power)	(Generalization of value commitments)
	The polity	Fiduciary institutions

Table 6.1

The four *means* refer to different qualities of the interacting persons. Among human beings there are some whose physical endowments suggest that it's best not to cross them; some who are charismatic and can always convince others of their own viewpoint; others who know how to make the most of existing resources; and others we respect for a high correspondence between what they believe and how they act. Parsons, however, stresses that each of these means has a symbolic dimension, meaning it does not refer exclusively to individual characteristics and capacities. For instance, the actor's intentions must somehow be communicated to others because such means can come into play; even the most brutal coercion would get nowhere without being previously known as a threat to the actor one wants to induce to do something. Again, even an actor's rewarding activity, to constitute an incentive for another, can assume a symbolic form, as with the promise of future actions or granting recognition or respect to others. Therefore, each means has a material basis, which can be presented and extended symbolically, as when we obey someone not because he frightens us but because we believe that, if we cross him, he will bring into play others who are much more violent than he is.

According to Parsons, this symbolic component allows actors to bring to bear on their own interactions many more resources than are materially available in their circumstances at a given moment. The capacity to formulate credible threats allows a measure of (coercive) control with respect to many more activities and

contexts than can be satisfactorily resolved by activating only one's own physical force. In the same manner, if one can count on other actors' sharing with us
certain kinds of values, this can ground much more trust in our relations than
can derive from each of us monitoring the others (their biographies, or their
interests) closely, before deciding to follow their advice.

The emphasis Parsons lays on the symbolic dimension of the means employed
within interaction serves to point out the relation between the sanctions operating
at this level and the functional requirements of the social system. The more significant the symbolic component of the various means, the greater the autonomy
of actors vis-à-vis their environment and the possibility of differentiating and
enriching the interactive experience. Those means are not fashioned ad hoc for
every single interaction; they keep circulating from one interaction to another.
The actor puts into play what Parsons calls *generalized means of interchange,* such
as money (incentive), power (coercion), influence (persuasion), and the appeal to
shared values (activation of values). Each actor may call on such means not with
reference to whatever interaction he is involved in but insofar as, and to the extent
that, they are available within whole networks of interaction. Even illegitimate employment of such means cannot be understood in purely isolated, individualistic
terms. It is only within a context where religion is highly valued that it pays for
scoundrels to present themselves as pious. Only in an advanced money economy
does it make sense to produce and deal in counterfeit money. With reference to
the most obviously significant means—money, whose centrality we have already
seen affirmed by Marx and Simmel—Parsons emphasizes the extent to which the
modern economic order depends on institutional arrangements that guarantee
the value of money, rendering the actor's spending decisions both possible and
binding. It is by way of money that the aggregation of the innumerable economic
choices of multiple actors generates significant effects for the economic subsystem of society, determining for instance the phenomenon either of deflation or
of inflation. At the same time, the situation of the economic system—that is, in
Parsons's terms, of the adaptive processes of the whole social system—opens up
or closes opportunities of interaction for the actors. For instance, it can allow
(or *not* allow) one of them to use money as an incentive to get the others to act
in the manner desired. Consequently, what appears to a given actor as a means
to personal ends operates at the institutional level as a set of conditions whereby
each separate interaction is coordinated with all other interactions.

This effect (here described in the most rudimentary manner) has long been known in the case of money. According to Parsons, however, similar effects can be imputed to all his "generalized means of interchange." Also, political power and influence circulate within society, and by the same token they can have an inflationary or deflationary effect on both the respective subsystems and the stability of society as a whole.

MODERN SOCIETIES

Parsons considers *modern society* in particular as an especially complex, sophisticated, mobile ensemble of conditional and normative components, structured by the coexistence of a plurality of specialized subsystems, each institutionalizing distinct values, norms, collectivities, and roles. This network of differentiated structures, and the resulting system of solidarity, is held together by a set of mechanisms that allow their reciprocal interdependency to persist while remaining flexible.

Parsons has no doubt that this specifically modern form of social organization not only is more efficient than previous ones but enjoys greater moral validity. On this count, he sharply criticizes those intellectuals who, associating themselves with a nostalgia for a mythically conceived past, tend to depict modern society as being constantly on the brink of collapse (hence the extended literature on the idea of decline in the West). On the contrary, in his view it represents a singular historical success. Modern society has established a high level of control over the material and cultural conditions of its existence (by augmenting its adaptive capacity), and at the same time it is able to institutionalize a high level of individual and social emancipation (through enhanced inclusion in a single integrative sphere).

Basically, for Parsons the advances in the process of structural differentiation characterizing modern society allow the social system to entitle all members to become legitimately included within its structure. This reifies a generalized, potentially universal membership he calls *citizenship*, which does not in principle depend on the individual's relationship to economic wealth, political power, or cultural tradition.

Such a view centers on one chief consideration. Parsons does not deny that, even in modern society, various processes uphold or assert positions of privilege, but he believes that society's advanced and progressive social differentiation necessarily breaks the matrix of predetermined expectations marking all premodern forms of social organization. They assigned all individuals a determinate status, whose various components were arranged within a hierarchically ordered system and generally inherited from one's parents. As opposed to this, the emergence of a plurality of differentiated structures makes it ever more unlikely for individual roles to remain perfectly aligned with one another, and for some individuals to obtain all favorable roles and others to attain all unfavorable ones. Here, with the advance of modernity, there unavoidably emerge strains and inconsistencies until it is no longer possible to predict and preordain all of an individual's behavior on the basis of his or her primary, ascriptive status. When such strain and incompatibility manifest more comprehensively, it becomes functionally mandatory to include all individuals within the society on the basis of shared rights, allowing vertical inequality only with reference to multiple, specific roles individuals hold within various collectivities.

According to Parsons, in modern societies such collectivities, given their growing involvement in diverse and inclusive structures, tend to behave according to universalistic and meritocratic criteria. Few politicians completely abandon a whole section of the electorate to opponents merely because they do not share religious convictions, and no firm easily surrenders a portion of its profit only to avoid dealing with the members of some ethnic minorities.

Thus for Parsons the differentiation process essential in modernity lays the conditions for an increased social dimension of equality and growing social mobility, although he acknowledges that other processes (such as the fact that families' locations in the socioeconomic hierarchy largely determine the educational path and the occupational choices of their children) constitute a hindrance to the full realization of true equality of opportunities. In his judgment, modern, differentiated societies can institutionalize levels of social mobility incomparably more dynamic than those attainable in premodern societies, and functional requirements and normative criteria of social justice closely interact in this process. This consideration characterizes what one may consider Parsons's political program: a committed defense of the profoundly moral character of modern society over against those who, from the left or the right, call for a process of de-differentiation. This also calls attention to the fact that modern society has not fully delivered on its promise, and that on a number of counts it has not taken the differentiation process far enough to realize its promise: a thoroughly universalistic and inclusive societal community.

7 ERVING GOFFMAN

Canadian sociologist with an anthropological background (1922–1982). Originally associated with symbolic interactionism, he developed a personal approach that also drew from other disciplines such as linguistics and ethology. His works were often the result of protracted observation of aspects of everyday life in disparate groups, such as islanders from the Shetlands, croupiers in Las Vegas, patients of a psychiatric clinic, and people spending time in public parks. He also used novels, TV shows, advertisements, and many other sources.

SUGGESTED READINGS
The Presentation of Self in Everyday Life, Anchor/Doubleday, Garden City, New York, 1978.
Asylums: Essays on the Social Situation of Mental Patients and Other Inmates, Aldine, Chicago, 1961.
Stigma: Notes on the Management of Spoiled Identity, Touchstone, New York, 1986.
Interaction Ritual: Essays on Face-to-Face Behavior, Pantheon, New York, 1982.
Frame Analysis: An Essay on the Organization of Experience, Northeastern University Press, Chicago, 1986.

MOST OF ERVING GOFFMAN'S ANALYSES deal, at the core, with the reasons and consequences of a well-known but relatively unexplored aspect of human sociality: that we never truly know who we are dealing with. Underdetermined by his inherited, biological equipment and possessing remarkable cerebral complexity, the social actor is not transparent. It is never possible to know precisely his intentions and to predict his actions. Within relatively long-lasting and intense social relations, we may feel that their unfolding can no longer reveal surprises. Yet even such relations may take a sudden, unpredictable turn; persons we are well acquainted with may show aspects we would not have thought existed, and many familiar, solid relations may retrospectively appear deceptive after a new development or revelation.

This does not hold true only for highly emotion-laden relationships. Many other human interactions take place within relatively well-established boundaries, where activities address specific demands and exchanges follow highly codified sequences. At least in such cases, one would not expect any surprises from interaction. But such an expectation can be suddenly falsified. The barman with whom we've always spoken briefly and casually about insignificant topics may suddenly go off on a passionate tirade relating to a new topic or even an old one, and make us lose minutes we intended to devote to drowning our sorrows or griping about our own problems. A colleague who had always behaved most civilly or indeed submissively may from one moment to the next become loud and aggressive. A friend we had always assumed to be not well off because he always complained about his financial condition may turn out to be rather wealthy.

When others reveal totally unexpected resources, tendencies, or concerns, the nontransparency of human beings comes into focus. Such trauma, however, is rather infrequent; generally the actors to whom we personally relate by and large behave as we expect them to. Thus our ability to understand others' actions is rarely challenged or shown to be problematic. The conversational exchanges in the bar previously mentioned are generally short in duration. In most of the course of human life, one is involved in routinely intelligible interactions, and social life transpires as "business as usual." How is it possible for actors who are nontransparent and potentially unpredictable to one another to enter and manage relations and interactions in ways that, on the contrary, seem stable, comprehensible, and predictable? All of Erving Goffman's numerous writings address this one basic question, to a somewhat varying extent and in differing manners.

According to Goffman, any kind of interaction requires the participants to control and communicate large amounts of information. Such information may be strictly personal in nature, concerning the other participants' particular needs, wishes, preferences, and resources. Sometimes we also need information concerning the social positions the participants occupy, since these determine just how much authority, influence, consideration, esteem, and respect they feel entitled to. It is often necessary to gain and use information relating to the biographical background of other participants because it may entail peculiar demands concerning how they are to be treated and the greater or lesser degree of consideration they receive. If we want to understand how interaction unfolds, we also need to know how such information becomes accessible in the course of it.

PRESENTATION OF SELF

Three main points are relevant here. First, information of all kinds has some bearing on interaction, and because it varies in quantity and quality so does the conduct of participants. Second, all actors have something they conceal, if only to the extent that this may assist them in presenting themselves in public as "better"—defined socially as more desirable or at least acceptable—than they are in fact. Even individuals possessing socially more desirable qualities do not actually possess all of them, and almost never fully. On this account, each actor is interested in the degree of control she has over the information available in the environment in which she operates concerning her person, intentions, resources, and capacities. Third, although such information is critical for interacting with someone else (in order to guess his intentions, to classify him as belonging to this or that category, to forecast his possible reactions to our own actions), it is never immediately and completely available within the interaction. Instead, it must be discerned by "reading" all manner of signals derived from present and previous experience, and by constructing more or less complex hypotheses.

Consequently, there is always a significant—and often major—gap between individuals' personal and social identities (as they would appear to a hypothetical and, unrealistically, fully informed observer) and how those identities are apprehended and taken into account by the actors involved in a given interaction. Contexts may vary considerably in the degree of detail with which they define the individuals' attributes and their bearing on the respective amount of power, prestige, or consideration due to them. Specific interaction participants may be more or less inclined and able to identify such attitudes and adopt an appropriate response. In any case, some information gap exists in every interaction, and participants must continuously interpret the other participants' actions in light of what may be observed in the unfolding interaction, by assuming they are both providing and withholding information and resources not immediately accessible there and then. Social interaction proceeds to the extent that all participants behave *as if* all actors were reciprocally transparent and *as if* the information directly or indirectly acquired in the course of interaction were sufficient and reliable. Goffman stresses that any form of human communication whatever presupposes this phenomenon. In the moment an actor utters a sentence, he must—at the risk of otherwise being deemed crazy—formulate it in a manner allowing it to be perceived as appropriate. In other words, he must establish a link between his own utterance and a whole ensemble of noninteractional premises he shares with those listening to him. By the same token, he excludes many other references to other premises that the listeners instead ignore. Furthermore, the utterance must be formulated such that the listener interprets it as revealing his own intentions, emotions, or condition.

As a result, the actor must be aware of, and refer to, what Goffman terms the *definition of the situation*: expectations implicitly shared by the participants. Similarly, an answer addressing someone else's question must be formulated so as to take into account not only individual statements one responds to but also the shared assumptions they evoke. If the jealous husband asks if you worked late, it is sometimes appropriate to reply not with a description of your work schedule but with reassurance that you are not seeing your lover anymore. This also applies beyond linguistic utterances. Every social action must not only correspond to a specific objective but also acknowledge the requirement that those witnessing it be able to interpret it. The action must be shaped to establish that the person engaged in it, whether or not her objectives are shared, is doing something meaningful. Even if an action is of a provocative or hostile nature, it must nonetheless be formulated to allow its targets to interpret it as a meaningful provocation or as an instance of hostility.

To communicate means to manifest a set of attributes, intentions, and competences to others. An information gap, then, implies the existence of an interactional space where attributes and intentions must be "presented" to other participants in a way that respects various requisites.

At any rate, in certain aspects social interaction must resemble a theatrical scene in which a script made of expectations compels actors, without binding them to a specific identity or text, to appear somewhat plausible. In other words, one is bound to act in a role, but there is a place for ad-libbing that allows one to choose among strategies of self-presentation. Goffman attaches much significance to the expression "social actor," with its implicit reference to the theatrical or, as he sometimes calls it, "dramaturgical" experience. Each of us, *qua* social actor, resides within a dense network of situations and encounters. Here the social actor, by means of his bodily and linguistic behavior, constantly expresses a stream of activities. They acquire meaning in light of the specific kind of situation and the expectations of the other participants.

Therefore a person conducting herself extremely informally will arouse suspicion if she is performing the function of a public official, whereas the same manner of conduct would be permitted or even required by this person in her night job as an entertainer in a tourist village. Yet it may be the case that an appropriately behaving official is in fact a con man, whereas an entertainer is in fact a properly trained, successful applicant for some public office.

Goffman emphasizes that each actor, within a network of interactions, must maintain a *face*, a self-image worked out and acted on with reference to behaviors and attributes that the other participants in the interaction deem pertinent and worthy of approval. To accomplish this, the social actor must orient himself to the expectations and preferences of his public, employ his knowledge of the relevant social scripts, and make appropriate use of the costumes and props available for the stage. In this manner, if successful he can establish a certain control over the information his own act makes available to the other actors. He can hide potentially damaging or embarrassing information, reduce possible inconsistencies between aspects of his persona and his acts, or emphasize the information that renders plausible his holding and performing a given role.

This *dramaturgical performance* idealizes the actor's presence and activity within the scene. If he performs it successfully, he conveys the meaning of his action by appearing insofar as possible as the living embodiment of an ideal model. When required, he can stress the coherence between his present and past actions, or between the role he occupies in this scene and those he occupies elsewhere. If discrepancies still appear, he can acknowledge them but impute positive significance to them, suggesting they are due to the fact that he is still learning and preparing himself. In other words, as they interact, actors act out the role of who they would preferably be, rather than who they are in the present. This dramaturgical capacity, according to Goffman, belongs, to a lesser or greater degree, not only to people occupying problematic roles—professional or amateur actors, con men, spies, cheaters of various kinds—but to *all* human beings in *all* their interactions.

On this account, he adopts an original methodological approach. Most social actors are not involved in show business, and very few of them operate professionally under circumstances requiring enactment of diverse identities. In spite of this, *all* social actors make use, more or less competently, of the techniques and strategies of theatrical actors. And vice versa: in a particularly self-conscious and explicit manner professional actors (and spies) employ a set of techniques and strategies of self-presentation grounded in those that the social actor adopts to confront and manage the most banal contingencies of social life.

Following up on this intuition, Goffman closely analyzes the techniques adopted by those with demeaning and humiliating attributes to reduce the impact of the attributes on their interactions. For instance, he studies the practices of individuals seeking to hide their sexual preference, or trying to conceal untoward aspects of their own past, or whose occupational careers have shown a marked downward trend. He derives from these inquiries valuable insights as to how human beings present themselves. It appears that the attempt to present oneself in the most favorable manner and to limit the negative import of one's damaging attributes in the eyes of others mobilizes the same interactional competences and the same devices of theatrical self-presentation.

It has long been known that human beings seek to place themselves in a favorable light by manipulating appearances, and for centuries this has been a constant source of concern for moral philosophers. Goffman evaluates the same phenomenon in a very different way. He does not view such processes of self-presentation as a morally dubious form of deception or denial of one's authentic self. On the contrary, such a place for self-presentation allows the very possibility of constructing the individual self. Our ability to manipulate our self-presentation opens up a space for moral freedom, not only for strategic choice, because it allows us to align to socially defined conditions for enjoyment of moral dignity and individual worth. As they seek to manipulate reality to project an acceptable image, actors are induced to adopt, unself-consciously, a ritual behavior whose upshot is to confirm and celebrate the appropriate moral order of a given society and context. Consider, furthermore, the part that certain social resources play in even making it possible to maintain a positive self-image. According to Goffman, the self is not a property bestowed on an individual in the course of interaction, but a model of relations addressed by both the individual's own action and the public validation his performance receives from other actors. The individual can construct and maintain a dignified self-image only if this model respects certain features.

To identify such conditions, Goffman studied closely and at length the interactions taking place (among other situations) within a psychiatric hospital, which he considered one instance of a broader category of social contexts that he labeled *total institutions* (other instances are prisons, monasteries, and military academies). Typically, these institutions control every aspect and moment of an individual's existence to compel him or her to undergo a change in personality. By analyzing the organization of the hospital, and the *career* the inmates followed while there, Goffman treated the individual strategies he observed as a kind of natural experiment, whereby he explored in some detail the structural requirements to be fulfilled to maintain a positive self-image.

To begin with, if one observes what individuals *lose* as they become inmates of a total institution, one realizes that in order to manage an image, however minimally dignified, individuals need to control at least some resources and space of autonomy (he calls this *territories of the self*). They must have under their own undisputed control at least a minimum number of objects, some space in which to escape constant monitoring by others, and some interactions allowing them a minimum of autonomy in how they represent themselves and in using appropriate means. Above all, for an actor to preserve or develop a positive identity, she should possess at least a few social attributes that all the participants in the interaction define in positive terms. If such conditions are not satisfied, for her to seek to maintain a dignified image of herself is not only very difficult but dangerous; it only makes her a candidate for escalating processes of humiliation. As a result of living a long time in these degrading conditions, the image of the self breaks down progressively and the individual learns little by little to practice (in Goffman's wording) *the amoral arts of shamelessness* (Goffman, 1961: 169).

Social interaction, however, cannot be reduced to a simple succession of individual self-presentations. Self-representation is not merely the product of the actor's role performance; it requires the audience to acknowledge the performance. Goffman views interaction as similar to a performance involving audience participation, where the public intervenes not only by assessing the effectiveness of the show but also by making inputs to the staging. The presentation of the self to participant audiences (including those involved only peripherally and occasionally) must correspond not only to what one is seeking to express but also to the kind of consideration one wants to elicit from others.

At the same time, the acting should be considered somewhat compulsory. Whenever one is in the physical presence of others, all participants will assume that one is communicating, whether or not one actually wants to communicate. To be indifferent to the impression one transmits to others does not prevent such transmission from taking place; rather, it means losing control over whatever impression others will develop of the actor. While taking part in an emotionally charged argument, one may happen to yawn, not for lack of involvement but rather because one has slept little the night before. However, if the yawn is not suppressed, or apologized for and otherwise explained, others will interpret it as expressing boredom or indifference and react accordingly. This also has further, not easily detected, implications. The other participants, in turn, are not transparent, and the meaning of their reactions to all behaviors may have rather different meanings. Suppose one bursts into tears during an encounter with one's partner; does the latter's affectionate reassurance express true empathy, or is it simply a way of bringing an embarrassing situation to a close? The resulting series of adjustments and confirmations is a central aspect of interaction, whereby all actors cooperate in keeping within the agreed boundaries of the situation.

The significance of this collaborative aspect for managing social interaction is particularly evident where presentation of self is connected to presentation of a collective identity. This happens particularly within organized social contexts, for here—within institutionally and sometimes physically separate boundaries—actors operate not so much as individual actors but (to maintain the metaphor) as actual theatrical companies with relatively stable composition. An office, a family, a gambling house are but a few instances of such contexts, where an ensemble of persons enduringly cooperate to project to a given audience a specific understanding of reality, of what they are about, and of why they operate in a particular manner. In such organized realities, actors accord presentation of their individual selves with the shared requirement of giving outsiders an impression of collective order and control.

Goffman emphasized that the twofold nature of such operation requires the existence and management of two distinct public spaces. One (the frontstage) is rendered visible to the audience and is where the actors jointly conduct a performance intended to suggest a strongly structured and formalized reality in which each enacts a precisely defined role. The other (the backstage) is where the same actors *organize* the performance out of view, manage unexpected contingencies, and hide the secrets that if visible on the stage would spoil the show. The backstage not only allows what happens in the presence of the audience to be prepared; it is also a stage in itself, where a different play goes on. Here the actors perform their solidarity with one another and above all stress the existence of a difference between the publicly performed roles and the self as revealed only to the other members of the troupe (which, all agree, is more "authentic").

THE INTERACTION ORDER

So far we have considered the joint effect on the one hand of the "obligation" to present oneself and on the other hand of the actors' reciprocal nontransparency. This combination brings about continuous tension because the effort of presenting oneself to others may well engender not cooperation but serious misunderstanding and open conflict. Yet this occurs fairly infrequently in the social experience of most actors. Why? Goffman answers that interaction consists in and presupposes the continuous operation of processes of *repair*—mending contingencies that would give away the game. Such processes in turn involve all participants. Above and beyond a particular script, there exists a set of moral norms controlling not only how to enter into mutual relations but also how to react to the incidents and mishaps that may arise from time to time.

For example, when previously unacquainted people meet, a set of detailed rules is activated, which, if observed, minimizes the occurrence of social relations that one or more participants do not want to occur. For instance, all those present in a public space—a street, a park, a bar—are aware that it behooves them not to make prolonged eye contact with one another, to present whatever visual or physical contact occurs as casual and unwanted, not to claim a right to evoke attention on the part of others. At the same time, all participants must consent to this system of rules to interact. To make this possible, some actors may be seen as constituting categories (for instance, the police members patrolling the park, the persons manning an information point) whose members can be contacted in legitimate and patterned ways. Or there may be conditions under which one can appropriately seek, directly or indirectly, to activate some kind of interaction. During a walk in a park one may address a child, hoping this disposes the parent to communicate, or one may pick up something a young woman has dropped with the intent of initiating conversation. Thus there are some strategies that initiate interaction, or vice versa that bring interaction to a close without creating offense. For instance, if we thank civilly but impersonally somebody's act of kindness, we may acknowledge it while signaling that we have no intention to prolong the interaction.

Now, such a system of rules lowers the probability of mistakes or misunderstanding, but of course it does not eliminate it. By this account, we must consider another crucial component of Goffman's argument, which amounts to a true process of interactional repair. There are rules allowing mistakes in communication to be remedied, as when interaction is initiated on the assumption that other participants are disposed to sustain it but successively this appears not to be the case; or when one unwillingly conveys an unwanted or contradictory message to others. There are two kinds of such norms, each performing its own functions. One enjoins participants to pay no more than minimal attention—to the extent of pretending one has not noticed—to an actor's behavior that can be considered unpleasant but involuntary (*civil inattention*). For instance, one pretends not to notice a sneeze that interrupts a conversation, or one signals with a smile that the sneeze presents no problem. The other kind (*forgiveness*) prescribes that whoever has done something problematical should acknowledge it as a mistake recognized as unpleasant. In this way, he is allowed to distinguish his "real" self from the one responsible for the problematic action, aligning himself with the moral position of whoever has witnessed it and is potentially offended by it, which makes it unjust to sanction it further. Taken as a whole, this system of rules fulfills a crucial function: to keep social action taking place in public spaces within parameters that minimize risk to the actors' claim to their own dignity, allowing them instead to represent themselves as socially competent and deserving of respect.

Even assuming all actors share the objective of a dignified presentation of themselves, this does not mean everyone can accomplish it to the same extent. On the contrary, Goffman insistently acknowledges a plurality of stratification arrangements that constantly, and sometimes emphatically, place actors into socially differentiated positions concerning how much respect, recognition, and consideration those occupying such positions receive from those occupying others. He emphasizes that the presentation of oneself is structurally connected with the access one has to certain social resources, which as a rule are unequally distributed among the participants. Access to them is directly proportional to the status of the members of society; those of higher status also have greater control over objects, enjoying greater privacy in their relations and greater autonomy in their interaction activities. Above all, to be at the top of status stratification entails a much smaller risk of experiencing disappointment and humiliation in one's self-presentation, since this is likely to reflect the highest and most sought-after values in the dominant culture. Contrarily, those whose attributes disqualify them from full membership in society—such as having been in jail, having a physical deformity, or being a closeted member of some despised category (all conditions of what Goffman calls *stigma*)—are continually compelled to act not in order to claim a public validation of their own moral status but, if anything, to reduce the risk of undergoing endless, wounding public disclosure and humiliation.

Into his analysis of such stratification processes, Goffman introduces two distinctive aspects of modern society that he views as critical for social interaction.

First, modern society does not institutionally separate actors on the basis of social attributes (there is a claim to putative equality), thus making less likely, within a given population, the development of alternative systems of distribution of social honor. As modern societies typically operate, every actor often finds himself in contact, say in public places, with individuals whose social attributes differ from his own, since there is no institutionalized separation of social classes. Furthermore, every actor may interact with participants who, as information accumulates about them or the situation changes, turn out not to have the social characteristics that, being previously taken for granted, had presided over the beginning of the interaction.

Second, it is not possible (as opposed to what happened in premodern societies) to treat actors occupying a lower status in a manner that legitimately echoes and affirms this status. As actors in possession of higher resources, they too share the same preferences, concerning dignity and honor.

This situation is historically unprecedented, and according to Goffman it generates recurrent risks for managing interaction because there is an endemic risk of being "out of place," in situations of unease, in a circle of people that we do not "belong" to. On this account, Goffman holds there is again a system of norms, which together with the continuous labor of repair keep the actors' interactional risks within tolerable limits.

There are less explicitly regulated situations, such as those occurring in public spaces. Here too, according to Goffman, status stratification affects the ease with which strangers access one another. At the bottom of the resulting hierarchy are those who Goffman calls *open persons*, individuals whom for a variety of social reasons anybody in a given public place can access without particular reservation or circumspection. At the top, instead, are actors whom one must beware of bothering in approaching them without being asked, on penalty of serious loss of social dignity. In between are a series of individuals to whom, on the strength of various aspects of their self-presentation—their *demeanor*—one may attribute a higher or lower disposition to enter into relations with oneself on the basis of (presumed) status similarity or inferiority. The "good manners" applying to such encounters in public places may allow one to initiate new relations with relatively little risk, among other reasons because if they turn out to be unsatisfactory one may withdraw in a way that does not entail conflict.

Even within relatively standardized relations, though, recognizing the actual status of individuals with whom one deals is a persistent problem. And even within rather strongly bounded contexts, such as organizations or professional bodies, one can derive only an approximate sense of the positions actors hold within the various relevant social stratifications, only from their self-representation or indirectly from the conduct of other actors toward them. Goffman observes that in the course of interaction one can ascertain only with difficulty a meaningful part of the subjects' previous life course. Often one would deal with people quite differently if one knew their itinerary preceding the beginning of the interaction. Even when interactions are repeated over time, the individuals involved may undergo considerable change in their relevant attitudes. As Goffman puts it, "The dead are sorted but not segregated, and continue to walk among the living" (Goffman, 1952: 463). When this happens, different strategies may be pursued. It is possible to practice a straightforward interruption, with more or less a show of indignation, of the interaction itself. Or it is possible to offer the interactional partner a lower position, congruent with suitable status given the recently acquired information, without depriving him of the chance to maintain some dignity. This option, as applies to an individual who has been the victim of a con game, is called by con men "cooling the mark out." A former executive may be offered the "more creative" role of consultant; a husband may accept the role of close confidant to his former wife.

In his later years, Goffman dealt at length with a final aspect of actors' nontransparency: how the actors establish the sort of interactions in which they involve themselves. How do they understand what kind of expectations they are about to confront? To address this question, Goffman points out the operation of an ensemble of symbolic entities—which he refers to as *frames*—each of which carves out of social experience a certain territory and addresses the attention of participants toward its identifying features. The metaphor points to the fact that a picture frame delimits a picture's boundaries and at the same time signals that it is a work of art and not a squiggle on the wall (a confusion that may be excused regarding certain kinds of contemporary visual art).

What one may call the frame effect, for instance, allows actors to distinguish between a natural event and a social one, a social interaction and its artistic representation, a joke and a bitter remark about human nature, training practice and the actual game. The notion of frames implies that the events one sees unfolding do not possess a once-and-for-all meaning or an "authentic nature" aside from how they are represented and interpreted. Goffman does not mean by this, and by his other analyses of interaction, that any social event can be interpreted whichever way one likes. The existence of frames and how they are employed depends highly on many factors and structural givens. Just as human perceptions are strongly constrained by the human body's biological features (we cannot hear certain sounds or perceive certain colors), so the variety and flexibility of symbolic frames is constrained by the organizational requirements of the interaction between human beings and by the possibilities opened—or excluded—by social organization. Just as the actors' self-presentations must be plausible, that is, *appear* realistic in the context of a given performance, so the symbolic frames cannot radically conflict with the actual conditions of social interaction in its settings. Goffman also comments on a certain degree of reciprocal autonomy between social conditions and symbolic frames, such that the latter may sometimes make certain forms of social organization more likely or instead put them in question.

THE NATURE OF THE INDIVIDUAL SELF

All that has been said so far naturally leads to a query: whether the individual self possesses an "authentic" nature, and if so what it may be. Goffman himself gave only somewhat ambiguous answers to this query. Various critics suggest that his texts point to two different selves coexisting: the one exhibited in public and socially validated, which we have mostly discussed so far; and one that can sometimes be found in his writings, a self-standing actor who lies behind or above and directs the public self. The latter self is the puppet-master, so to speak, of the public self, manipulating its behavior on stage to pursue his own closely held ends.

By and large, anyone reading Goffman can easily see that his analyses do not refuse to recognize the individual as an entity made of flesh and blood (and capable of complex neural operations). He also frequently acknowledges the individual's aspiration to control the environment and pursue some degree of social success. He seems fully aware that the subjects involved in interactions bring to them preexisting biographies of their own, which impinge on the interactions they enter into. Finally, he stresses some universal characteristics of human beings, such as the ability to foresee, desire, suspect, and fear; and some tendencies, such as avoiding shame and embarrassment and feeling at ease. At the same time, however, Goffman sees no reason to hold that these facts, and the analyst himself partaking of human nature, require us to impute to such individuality a higher scientific standing than one that may result from adopting other viewpoints. That individuals exist does not necessarily place them at the center of theoretical or empirical inquiry.

Goffman argues this in two mutually independent but compatible lines of discourse. First, he remarks that whoever aims to construct a philosophical anthropology unavoidably produces a "Man" with features so universal and generic that they have little bearing on what actual human individuals have experienced and sought in a given place and time. In Goffman's own words, "Universal human nature is not a very human thing" (1955: 45). What is sociologically of interest takes place at specific points within the extraordinary range of possibilities opened up by an anthropological perspective.

A second position concerns the proper status to attribute to the individual within *analysis* of social interaction. Here Goffman distinguishes clearly between two empirical facts: (1) that individuals preexist interaction and are to an extent autonomous with respect to it and (2) that within any course of interaction we continuously *assume* the preexistence of actors with a previous biography and a certain degree of autonomy. According to Goffman, the similarity between (1) and (2) is deceptive. Saying that individuals are not generated by social interaction is sensible. It does not change the fact that the presence and significance of the individuals *in* any given interaction is defined interactionally, and features of the preexisting individuals are noticed and made meaningful only as they play a role in the interaction. For instance, in almost all human interactions it is presupposed that the participants are all equally human, possess intentions and objectives, and thus have, as one currently phrases it, subjectivity. As a consequence, a variety of signals—bodily gestures, movements, verbal utterances, even how one clothes oneself and the posture one takes—are regularly interpreted as revealing the individual's subjectivity, no matter the actual reasons for the presence of these signals or the meaning such signals have for the person carrying them. In other words, it is how the actor performs his role that leads the audience to identify it as a *self*, as a specific actor endowed with preferences, intentions, skills, and moral standing. Whether and to what extent such features identified by the audience actually express the preference, intentions, skills, and moral standing of a given human organism becomes an *interactional* problem only as such difference may trigger processes leading to validating or discrediting the actor. If an audience with high expectations is disappointed by one of your performances, it does not help to claim that they should not have had such high expectations in the first place, or to stress that nothing was done to generate such expectations.

Goffman emphasizes that the frequent situations where a contrast between one's role and one's authentic self emerges may in turn be interactions in which the script allows the actor to double himself in two distinct roles, opposed to one another yet equally performed. *Within the analysis of interaction*, as Goffman sees it, the objective is not to depict the actor's own organic and psychical processes—to which the participants in the interaction have no access whatsoever—but rather the processes that make a given presentation of self credible for the participants. Audiences recognize (that is, attribute) subjectivity in the actor and judge it "authentic" or "fake" on the basis of his performances and of the interactionally available knowledge, not by accessing his "true" nature. In the same vein, from the standpoint of interaction the actor's previous biography certainly makes a difference, because biographies include more or less significant elements that may affect the plausibility of an interactional presentation. These biographical elements are significant only so long as they fit the requirements of interaction, increasing predictability, supplying stage props, making more credible threats or inducements, offering evidence for praise or denunciation, and so on.

From such a stance, it is perhaps possible to deduce a kind of political program (although Goffman was careful not to articulate it). Instead of claiming

abstract rights for abstract individuals, one should instead oppose those processes (described by him in some detail), which deprive some individuals of what
they need for presenting their own self in the ways that preserve their personal,
interactional dignity.

REFERENCES

Goffman, Erving, "On Cooling the Mark Out: Some Aspects of Adaptation to Failure,"
    in *Psychiatry*, 15(4), 1952, 451–463.
Goffman, "On Face-Work: An Analysis of Ritual Elements in Social Interaction," in
    Psychiatry, 18(3), 1955, 213–231.
Goffman, *Asylums: Essays on the Social Situation of Mental Patients and Other Inmates*,
    Aldine, Chicago, 1961.

8 HAROLD GARFINKEL

American sociologist (1917–2011). Having completed his Ph.D. at Harvard University, he spent most of his academic career at the University of California, Los Angeles (where he was Professor Emeritus until his death). He is known as the founder of a controversial research tradition called "ethnomethodology." He has published comparatively little for a sociologist of his standing, preferring a teaching style centered on seminars in which students are requested to carry on personally in their lives, experiments, and exercises.

SUGGESTED READINGS

Studies in Ethnomethodology, Prentice-Hall, New York, 1967.
Ethnomethodology's Program: Working out Durkheim's Aphorism, Rowman & Littlefield, Lanham, Maryland, 2002.
Seeing Sociologically: The Routine Ground of Social Action, Paradigm, Boulder, Colorado, 2006.
Toward a Sociological Theory of Information, Paradigm, 2008.

H AROLD GARFINKEL grounds his sociological analyses in two significant assumptions concerning the nature of social actors. First, they are animals thirsting for *meaning*; second, their conduct is inspired chiefly by a strong urge to "do the right thing" and not to find themselves "out of place" or inadequate, with a poor fit to their circumstances.

Garfinkel sees social actors, whatever their biographies and intents, as being compelled to ask themselves continuously (though not always consciously) how to make sense of the situations in which they find themselves, and of the other actors in it. They may be induced to interact from the most diverse and contrasting motives. Every actor in every situation, though, aspires first to become part of a mutually understandable interaction (or, as he puts it, of an *orderly* one). As we shall see, realizing this aspiration is not as simple a task as it may seem. Interpretation, as it is usually understood, is not sufficient. Entering any situation at all, even a banal one, or one with which they are well acquainted, actors must deal with the problem of how to produce actions that other participants may recognize as such.

This aspiration to have their actions recognized as pertinent is a key feature of the interactional space. All actors seek to indicate visibly and concretely that their own presence and actions are coherent and possess meaning in the context of the situation in which they are involved; but only other participants can recognize that this is the case. Each actor therefore undertakes lines of action that, insofar as they are perceived as congruent with the situation, allow others to recognize his presence as "natural," legitimate, or relevant (although they may or may not welcome it). In Garfinkel's theory, this ongoing attempt to attain such recognition is considered significant from both a factual and a moral perspective; it is required for interaction to take place, but it is also the object of an implicit expectation the violation of which may arouse in actors strong emotional reactions.

THE PROBLEM OF MUTUAL COMPREHENSION

All of Garfinkel's analyses address a fundamental question: How do participants and observers view and manage social life as a complex of coherent and orderly situations in which one can almost always orient oneself and that one may meaningfully describe to third parties? In the course of diverse activities and within various contexts, participants may experience consensus or dissent, find themselves involved in significant or insignificant activities, and feel gratified or frustrated. This can happen only within situations whose meaning we and others can comprehend. In the course of a single day, every actor traverses hundreds of situations that are different and sometimes unprecedented, and yet clearly distinct from one another and engendering diverse interactions. What is striking, according to Garfinkel, is that mostly we traverse such situations without even devoting much attention to them. At the end of the day, we may feel we have not had any remarkable experience. For instance, if we go to a movie we can easily comprehend that the men and women at the theater entrance are not merely talking to one another—though in fact some may be doing just that—but actually are in line for tickets. We do this even if we have not visited that theater before or if on that particular day there is a disorderly ticket line.

In fact, this mystery about social life fascinates Garfinkel. How is it possible for a multitude of mutually independent individuals, each possessing a sensorial apparatus, schemes of cognition, and evaluation of reality of his own and potentially quite unique to himself, in spite of all this to experience the social world as essentially shared and comprehensible? What makes social life so com-prehensible? How do the actors understand a given situation, at a given time, and in a given place, as a situation of a certain nature?

To address this question, Garfinkel precludes "explanations" that, in spite of their appearing plausible and being widely accepted by sociologists, he deems inadequate. According to some, what renders social reality orderly and under-standable is the extent to which social actors refer to previously experienced situations. For instance, I recognize that people gathered in front of a ticket of-fice make up a line because I have previously joined other lines to buy a ticket. According to others, the social world is comprehensible because actors share a system of norms defining various situations and instructing them how to be-have within each one (in this case, "Get in line!") and those who don't comply are ill-educated. According to still others, actors observe situations and gather information as to what and how they act in view of their objectives (a poster over the ticket window effectively states "To get a ticket, form a line").

Naturally, Garfinkel does not consider such explanations wrong. Actors do refer to previous situations that render the present one more or less familiar, refer to norms and expectations that account for the unfolding of an interaction, and collect information concerning their social circumstances. Furthermore, he emphasizes that when asked how they manage to operate within a given situa-tion, actors will almost always appeal to one or more of those explanations. He holds, however, that none can adequately account for the shared understand-ing achieved in social situations. Previous experience does not guarantee that it will reliably reproduce itself, because situations may change; the ticket office may have been moved, or new ways of distributing tickets may have been intro-duced. Suppose, for instance, that on arriving at the theater people are expected to collect a numbered token from an automatic machine; insisting on stand-ing in front of the cash window would gain no one priority, whether or not he has been waiting under the theater canopy longer than someone who has just collected a token from the machine. In such cases, to invoke a right based on previous experience would be considered contrary, or at best simple-minded.

Furthermore, many situations we approach may appear similar to those pre-viously experienced without being identical; what we know about movie theater lines may apply also in the case of concerts, public offices, and other experi-ences. In all such cases, previous experience can guide us only if we acknowledge those other circumstances as being "of the same kind" as lining up for a movie. In managing even the most banal situation, social actors cannot simply reproduce action sequences derived from previous experience.

Referring to acquired knowledge of the systems of norms regulating different situations may bring up analogous difficulties. To show this, Garfinkel planned a number of simple but clever experiments. The subjects did not know that he was arranging to alter some basic expectations designed to test Parsons's notion of expectation. Such experiments demonstrated that even in the most standardized situations—say, a game of chess or checkers—it is possible to generate a variety of interactional events not envisaged by the rules of the game but that cannot be easily perceived as violating them. In other words, the most elaborate and comprehensive systems of norms cannot "describe" all that may happen. Furthermore, any expectation whatever requires that the event we are witnessing be acknowledged as such as to make the norms relevant. For instance, it is all right to show annoyance at a spectator who tries to jump the line, but one makes a bad showing if one does so when an usher is accompanying relatives of the performing artists to their reserved seats. No system of rules can cover all possible events, and every rule has its exceptions.

Garfinkel also stresses that actors generally make use of norms after events have taken place, rather than before. Norms are rarely invoked to orient oneself in the midst of a situation, whereas this regularly happens—to the extent of people assuming they exist even when not publicly declared and sectioned—in dealing with difficult events or forms of conduct.

Similar considerations apply to information or instructions. Here Garfinkel emphasizes the impossibility of specifying wholly exhaustive guidelines capable of automatically guiding an actor within a situation, no matter how straightforward. First of all, as is known to anybody who has tried to put together a chair by following the instructions from IKEA, guidelines are unavoidably selective; they omit as irrelevant a variety of aspects of the situation that may instead be of great practical significance. Furthermore, guidelines cannot take into account the turbulence characteristic of real interaction contexts, unforeseen developments, and the sudden relevance of extraneous criteria. No set of public instructions concerning how people should form a line at a ticket booth in a movie theater can include an indication that they do not apply in case of fire or riot, or the opening of a new booth, or days when entrance is free, and so on for an open-ended, possibly infinite series of considerations and unexpected events. Finally, it is not only a question of "discovering" and adapting to what is going on in the situation. Unforeseen developments do not simply induce the participants in an interaction to realize, however unwillingly, that they have not "properly understood" what was going on. Instead, they often arouse rage, indignation, and moral condemnation directed at those viewed as having caused such events.

In spite of this theorizing, all those reading this book at some point have joined and routinely join lines for tickets without encountering or causing particular difficulties. In fact, by doing so they have had recourse to rules and norms, have acquired information, and have followed instructions. Garfinkel asks how such resources are actually put to use and what confers on actors the real ability to acknowledge and reproduce an understandable and understood social world.

Garfinkel's own analyses argue that all such attempts to account for the comprehensibility of the social world cannot satisfactorily perform the task, for a very simple reason. They take for granted an individualistic, subjective understanding of the meaning of the social world; they focus exclusively on what the actors entering a given situation "know" and "expect." Therefore they do little else than reproduce as explanations of interaction those very views and assumptions the actors themselves employ to give others and themselves an account of their actions. According to Garfinkel, this is a fundamental mistake, which in fact hinders adequate understanding of social interaction.

In Garfinkel's perspective, the actors' experiences, expectations, and information are not considered "causes" of the comprehensibility of the interaction. They undoubtedly constitute resources (bodily, sensorial, cognitive, interpretive, evaluative competencies) indispensable for participation in social life, but they do not determine the unfolding of social interaction. Thus, Garfinkel starkly asserts, studying the social order does not require looking at what goes on in the actor's head, where all we would find is a brain. Instead, one must consider the place where the social order—the shared intelligibility of the situation—is continuously and concretely produced: the social situation itself, the interaction among a plurality of independent actors.

THE SOCIAL NATURE OF UNDERSTANDING
According to Garfinkel, a context is engendered wherever and whenever actors find themselves in one another's presence (or in any other situation involving

other actors). Their co-presence automatically leads each actor to try to forecast the others' reactions, taking their presence into account in his own conduct (if only by deciding to ignore them). Furthermore, mere physical co-presence pressures them to make their presence intelligible to the others. Such pressure, unavoidably turning physical co-presence into a social situation, derives from the anthropological perspective we have already emphasized: each participant is induced to forecast what the others will do, interpreting it as behavior endowed with meaning necessitating further behavior, which others in turn will consider meaningful. Even if the mutual knowledge of the actors is minimal, they must orient their bodies within the physical and social space and consider the presence of others in acting (if I look in a given direction, X may assume I am looking at her; if I look in another, she may assume I am trying to avoid her). Consequently, there is a compulsion to take meaning into account, such that actors are oriented, without necessarily focusing on it, to assume that any event is meaningful or socially intelligible (even when this is not the case).

Garfinkel's experiments yield a fundamental result: an actor may perceive a behavior or event as wrong, unjustified, or mad—but not as meaningless. As he writes, "The big question is not whether actors understand each other or not. The fact is that they do understand each other, that they will understand each other, but the catch is that they will understand each other regardless of how they would be understood" (Garfinkel, 1952: 367).

Co-presence becomes communication because whoever takes part in an interaction cannot help producing behavior that others will interpret in light of the specific features of the context. In any case they will impute meaning to the observed behavior of others. On the basis of physical co-presence, interaction takes on an orderly and intelligible character—to a greater or lesser extent, in a more or less continuous manner—sequentially, as the participants in the situation develop a level of shared understanding sufficient to allow the activities of any one to be interpreted by the other participants as being consistent with the view of the actor and of the context. As the participants in an interaction can foresee how others will interpret their own behavior, assuming for each participant the same interpretative capacity, a shared social world emerges where each can be held accountable for his own behavior (as Garfinkel phrases it, in this situation the mutual behavior attains *natural validity*).

To Garfinkel, the social world appears as a huge set of situations (*local social scenes*) all traversed by populations of actors entering and remaining for a shorter or longer time, committing themselves to more or less demanding activities. Such situations preexist before they enter and survive after they exit. All scenes share only one thing: they do not prescribe specific behavior but require all participants, continuously and compellingly, to induce the others to recognize their own presence as endowed with meaning and, as we shall see, accountable in light of contextual background expectations. Such situations render the events taking place within them observable and recognizable (by both participants and bystanders) as meaningful events only within the given context. (Anyone waving a butcher knife in the middle of a ticket line must be crazy, *but* he could also be someone hired to promote a horror movie.) In such interaction processes, the participants, while acting in such a way as to make other participants recognize and interpret their own presence as congruent with a given situation, continuously reproduce it. (I acknowledge what I am confronted with as a ticket line by placing myself behind the last person to join it, and in this manner I induce whoever comes next to recognize it as a line.)

We may appreciate why Garfinkel dissents from those who appeal to normative expectations in accounting for conduct. As we have mentioned, he does not deny that shared expectations perform a key role in interaction. He holds, however, that such a role does not consist in guiding actors as they evaluate what is taking place and in determining the appropriate response. The social expectation that has a fundamental bearing on the unfolding of interaction is, according to him, the generalized conviction that the situation *is* intelligible and that *therefore* each event may be traced back, more or less directly or tortuously, to a reason and a rule. Accordingly, actors treat events that compromise the comprehensibility of interaction as violations of the norms relevant to the situation, even if such norms have not been previously expressed or defined. By doing so, they reinforce understanding of the interaction as something rendered intelligible by the sharing of rules. Again, the unfolding of a meaningful situation turns out to depend on the prediction that all events take place according to rules, not on the content of the rules themselves.

This view of interaction leads Garfinkel to oppose attempts to understand the social order by reference to individualistic, subjective phenomena. Once they have come into being, situations affect actors as if from outside, not just because their structure strongly limits what one can accomplish by acting but for a deeper reason. The situation renders action (and the actor) intelligible, not the other way around. The dynamic nature of interaction selects the individual features that can be called on to interpret and describe the actor's conduct; the situation establishes which kinds of action are relevant and which are irrelevant, inadequate, or wrong. The actor's intentions make a difference to interaction only when successfully conveyed to other participants in an appropriate form, or when those participants impute them to the actor in order to make sense of unexpected behavior. Of course, Garfinkel does not deny that actors may have intentions prior to engaging in interaction; but they can be carried out only if they are rendered recognizable (and intelligible) to other participants in forms befitting a given situation. Every intention can be pursued only to the extent that all the participants engage in continuous and shared interpretations, such that interaction remains at least minimally coherent.

As a result, participation in any situation at all is possible only in the presence of specific patterns of interaction and perception. Once a situation has developed, how can its mutual and shared understanding be maintained in the face of the persistent possibility of divergent tendencies and of widespread opportunities for disagreement, ambiguity, and innovation?

According to Garfinkel, only the concurrence of a huge number of continuous activities of communication, perception, and evaluation makes interaction intelligible. The unfolding of the situation requires much maintenance and mutual adjustment. By emphasizing the process nature of order and its persistent dependence on activities of interpretation and normalization that make mutual action recognizable and intelligible, however, he implicitly postulates problematic situations, and the risk that the process itself fails to guarantee a sufficiently shared situation. All the members may aspire to be perceived as competent participants in the situation, but not all manage to do so. Even failure to attain a sufficient mutual comprehension does not necessarily lead to a collapse in interaction. On the contrary, wherever a situation is defined as endowed with meaning it places the participants under a normative expectation to take responsibility for keeping the interaction going, and to repair whatever disadvantages and defects may occur. Thus, although the actors do not necessarily derive their own conduct from normative expectations, they perceive as normative the definition of the situation and feel morally obligated to advance and respect it, and have others respect it.

Garfinkel also holds that even in the most stable and repetitive situations the social order is not grounded in habits or in shared values and criteria for action. It is, rather, rooted in the sharing, normatively expected, of the same *ways* of interpreting and managing events in light of the definition of the situation. It is on these grounds that Garfinkel labels *ethnomethodological* his own inquiries. It is an expression of his own coinage that warrants some unpacking. The reader may have already encountered terms such as ethno*botany,* referring to partitioning and characterizing forms of plant life shared within a given population, or ethno*history,* referring to ways in which a given population classify shared narratives and past events. When anthropologists and explorers use these terms, they imply that every member of the population is (also) a botanist and a historian, though mostly in a "lay" sense. These expressions suggest that about certain orders of phenomena a minimum patrimony of knowledge and competence, although differing from one population to another, is shared within each. In the same fashion, Garfinkel coined the expression ethno*methodology* to suggest that there also exists a patrimony of ways for all actors, mostly unself-consciously and in a lay fashion, to ascertain, classify, evaluate, and interpret other people's activities, rendering various situations mutually orderly and intelligible. The existence of these shared methods is what makes social order possible; members employ them to normalize incongruities, or to account for unexpected events in ways that are compatible with the assumption that the situation is intelligible.

According to Garfinkel, the situation makes such methods available; they can be seen in operation, learned, and adapted to particular times and places. Those taking part in a situation share not only a given set of tools for making their own actions recognizable, interpreting the actions of others, and confronting varying contingencies. They also share the sense that such methods are natural, taken for granted, and wholly adequate to needs, to the point where their occasional failure may be imputed not to the deficiencies of the tools themselves but to exceptional (and as a rule adverse) circumstances. At the root of such methods, we encounter once more the constitutive expectation that situations and events are *in any case* endowed with meaning. On this account, any action or event is perceived by actors as expressing an underlying meaning that may be interpreted in light of the shared understanding of the interaction in which one takes part. (Garfinkel calls such competence the *documentary method of interpretation.*)

Ensuring the intelligibility of the situation requires, then, a double movement. On the one hand, the extraordinary multiplicity of meanings that can be attached to what takes place is jointly viewed by participants as expressing a meaningful exchange intrinsic to the situation itself; on the other, each event is seen as conveying and confirming the shared definition of the situation. Garfinkel explored these double movements by conducting a particularly inspired and ingenious experiment, which he organized by means of a fake psychological service to the students of his own university, operated by experimenters directed by Garfinkel himself. The students, who thought they were availing themselves of assistance, could talk to an experimenter whom they assumed to be an expert in psychotherapy, and receive an answer to questions they asked; but the answer to each question could only take the form of a *yes* or a *no*, with minimal variants. Furthermore, the experimenter gave one or the other answer totally at random, paying no attention to question content but simply reading down a prearranged list of *yeses* and *nos* and offering it as his own comment.

As one can imagine, anybody reading a transcription of the resulting dialogue would find any number of implausible and incompatible answers. However, the students, perplexed as they might be concerning at least some answers to their questions, managed to see them as meaningful, as properly addressing their questions and capable of inspiring useful reflection. Therefore, as Garfinkel interpreted the findings, the unknowing victims of the deception revealed a marked capacity for "normalizing" basically incoherent and mystifying answers by assuming that the experimenter gave them in the role of a psychological counselor.

One may well feel that such results are the product of a markedly artificial setting. But Garfinkel obtained comparable findings from other experiments, regarding much more humdrum situations involving not subjects volunteering to avail themselves of such a service but participants operating within established, routine situations and fully aware of one another. For instance, over a period of time Garfinkel asked his own students to transcribe as literally as possible the brief, ordinary conversations of other members of their own family. The first result of this exercise was to realize that most such conversations were wholly incomprehensible from the transcripts. For instance, a father may report that his young daughter placed a coin in a parking meter while receiving from her mother an answer apparently having to do with getting a pair of shoes repaired—and so on. One could make sense of such conversations only by interpreting them in light of a sizeable body of shared and taken-for-granted understandings. In this case, the daughter had grown tall enough to reach the coin slot; the car had been parked, which pointed to the possibility—to be confirmed—of stopping at the cobbler's; and so on. What made such conversations comprehensible was not only the availability of a relatively large body of shared information but also—and perhaps above all—the reference to a wide gamut of implicit assumptions and presuppositions each participant imputed to the others. In other terms: the conversations could continue only insofar as all speakers took for granted that whoever the speaker addressed would understand and interpret his or her own interventions in the framework of such comprehension.

According to Garfinkel, this entails that the meaning of such conversations must not be sought exclusively or even primarily in the actor's intentions, in what she seeks to communicate. Rather, it is a product of the organization and unfolding of the interaction. The sequential ordering of the communications produces the meaning of an individual's statement. Indeed, this sequence confers meaning on the items in the conversation; what the actor "intends" to communicate appears to be endowed with meaning only insofar as it elicits the appropriate response from the others. Each communication constitutes a selection made from an irreducible plurality of possible meanings. Such interactional selection takes place at each and every moment in the communication process. The actor conveys her communication on the basis of her own understanding of the setting and anticipation of the others' interpretations. The others assume that what the actor communicates is endowed with meaning, and *consequently* they treat her communication as a message to be interpreted with reference to a broad ensemble of implicit knowledge assumed to be shared. The actor interprets the others' reactions as referring to the same criteria of significance and as being made comprehensible by a network of expectations congruent with her own message. At this point, the actor can intervene to correct or further qualify what she is communicating.

Garfinkel emphasizes that this construction of meaning does not lead to an "objective" end point but is always an ongoing process. At any time, a communication can lay bare a previous misunderstanding or open up a new order of possibility. This ongoing process can, of course, be considered one of *learning*, but the learning in question cannot be interpreted in purely cognitive terms. It is rooted in, and made possible by, only the participants' shared normative expectation that all actors involved are competent to communicate and interpret. Garfinkel sought to exclude such an expectation in some of his experiments. He asked his experimenters to require those with whom they spoke to express themselves as precisely as possible when making statements, but their unwitting subjects generally responded angrily and disdainfully, as if it was an offensive demand. One student asked an acquaintance to clarify what he meant by "How are you?" Did he want to know how he was physically, relationally, or psychologically? The reaction was not an appreciation for the capacity of the student to disentangle the various dimensions of well-being, but rather an angry reaction, concluding with an invitation to "drop dead." In other words, interaction participants expect to understand and be understood both as a matter of anticipating actual developments *and* as the holders of a morally grounded claim. The request of clarification by the student was perceived not only as inappropriate but also as morally outrageous, as a gratuitous offense.

This does not mean that the members of a situation are all in the same condition, entitled to the same prerogatives. On the contrary, there is often inequality in the ordering of interaction, different actors bringing to it qualities and resources of their own. It is not simply a matter of actors entering interaction with a varying patrimony of attributes—economic capacity, power, status, and so on—affecting what they can accomplish and how they are treated. Rather, according to Garfinkel, the conditions of participation in interaction vary with the individual, according to his or her vulnerability, that is, according to what the person has at stake in the interaction, what would be gained or lost should the interaction cease. The more fragile their interactional competence and the more uncertain their qualification to interact, the more important it becomes for them merely to uphold and assert the legitimacy of their participation in the interaction, above and beyond attainment of recognition and other specific objectives.

This argument is best developed in Garfinkel's highly research-grounded account of the case of Agnes. This subject presented herself to a clinic to change sex and thus conform her body to the female identity she already successfully practiced in social life. On the basis of this research, Garfinkel showed how even one's gender identity, far from being exclusively a factual matter, can be sustained only by practicing socially shared methods that make it understandable and significant in the context of interaction. (This insight has since been widely shared and indeed is currently rather taken for granted.) Agnes made a point of expressly and consciously learning and practicing such methods, and on this account she became an invaluable source of relevant information. By the same token, Garfinkel emphasized the enormous sacrifices required to attain such interactional success; Agnes had to avoid any situation that entailed risk of being uncovered, and devote to the innumerable aspects of the project a great deal of concentration and attention (continuously programming and monitoring ways of being and acting that most women adopt as a matter of course). On this account, she unavoidably experienced much profound existential anxiety.

Agnes did not confront such sacrifices in a spirit of rebellion; nor did she reject the gender differences codified by society. Far from it, Garfinkel stresses; Agnes was a firm believer in the natural character and justness of such differences, and she considered her efforts and sacrifices a way of manifesting her own compliance with the related gender demands. In later studies, Garfinkel went back to his original treatment of the Agnes case and argued that every situation reveals a strong distinction between "competent participants" (who in turn vary in degree of competence) and "novices." The former take for granted their own ability to put to competent use the methods required for their participation (and assume that such competence will be acknowledged by other participants); novices such as Agnes need to invest much more time and energy in observing others and themselves, and give priority to acquiring interactional competence over the pursuit of their personal objectives. The resulting inequality is more glaring if one considers that the status of "competent inter-actant"—even in apparently highly structured and ideologically universalistic situations—is conferred not as a matter of objective registration and recognition of competence but of a discretionary acknowledgment forthcoming from those already qualified as competent. Only when the usual range of application of shared methods is radically abandoned is this expressly noted and interpreted as deviant conduct. Aside from "novices" (induced by their fear of error to monitor their behavior continuously), competent members appeal naturally to those shared methods without focusing on them. They find them embodied in practices and habit warranting only minimal attention on their part. Therefore, the unfolding of these activities of interactional adjustment is governed not so much by the actors as by the interaction. Taking place within a sequence of communications, the process ensures that the meaning of an action is thematized and considered in light of the ensuing reactions, and in this manner it activates further action.

ACTIONS AND THEIR ACCOUNTS

This raises an interesting problem: social actors constantly talk about what they are doing and devote considerable time and energy to reporting, describing, and explaining their past, current, and future activities. A sizeable component of the shared methods actors use to operate in mutually understandable ways consists in linguistic devices allowing participants to present plausible retrospective accounts of why things happened a certain way. Garfinkel insistently argues that such explanations or accounts are a dimension of action radically different from those they claim to describe and interpret. What takes place, in fact, is not so much a linguistic summary of an event as a new event that recalls the previous one but also transforms it. One must distinguish the form of the actor's experience in the course of interaction—largely unself-conscious and derived from being part of a sequence of socially ordered events—from the form of a retrospective account of the same experience. Here the actor projects himself as an abstract third party vis-à-vis himself, recounting what has taken place in such a way as to make the action outcome intelligible, by referring it to an institutionally defined complex of motives, alternatives, and expectations. To this end, he employs a generalized vocabulary of motives and descriptions to make sense also for those who have not taken part in the interaction. Although the meaning of a situation is never a predictable product of interaction, within accounts whatever has taken place is retold as the natural outcome of its premises.

Such explanations matter a great deal both as a device for managing interaction, when offering one is the most frequent way of normalizing a communicational incident ("Excuse me, I did not greet you because I didn't see you"), and as an account of one's own conduct rendered to a variety of outsiders. Indeed, anyone who is part of a situation must appear intelligible and adequate in light of the expectations not only of the other participants but also of a range of other actors and audiences. For example, every year one must render the Internal Revenue Service an account of a whole set of monetary transactions, while what has happened during a business outing must be accounted for—generally in quite different terms—to one's spouse or one's coffee room associates. According to Garfinkel, the impact of institutions on social interaction can be detected in how they all require and prescribe distinctive ways, each relevant chiefly to a given institutional context, of accounting for what has taken place.

Garfinkel's analyses, beginning with those we have summarized here, have many diverse and significant implications for the study of social behavior, which have evoked a great deal of comment and controversy. The importance of this may be summarized by saying that a considerable number of practicing sociologists would see no reason for including this particular author among those we have been considering. One can understand such a frequently and sometimes vigorously advanced judgment (with which, needless to say, we disagree) by considering briefly how radically Garfinkel dissents from, and more or less explicitly criticizes, many established approaches to social research, both quantitative and qualitative, as well as many theoretical positions within sociology. One may differently assess such criticisms but should acknowledge if not their validity then their relevance, because they are closely entwined with how Garfinkel views social reality. We have seen the distance he posits between actors' actions, whose meanings and reasons lie only within the context in which they take place, and the accounts they offer of their actions to a variety of institutional subjects (including researchers). Furthermore, recall that according to Garfinkel the activities by which the members of a situation engender mutual behaviors and interpret them in mutually understandable ways entail processes of perception and interpretation they do not consciously learn or articulate conceptually, instead finding them embodied in taken-for-granted habits and practices. In considering this, one may easily understand the suspicion with which ethnomethodologists regard research approaches focusing on collecting actors' retrospective accounts, be they answers to formal questionnaires, probing and in-depth interviews, or extensive life histories.

What occasions such suspicion is not only the fact that social actors may lie or have imperfect recollection. The problem is that all such accounts unavoidably express a subjective, actor-centered viewpoint, whereas the social order, as Garfinkel sees it, lies entirely in the process and interactive dimension of action leading participants to adopt (in a sequential and embodied way) the methods shared by those taking part in a context. Actors do not *describe* such methods in their actual employment (for they are embodied in ordinary activities) but according to how the actors presume they work (thus, from the viewpoint of their outcomes). On the contrary, Garfinkel contends that one can study the social order only by observing directly what takes place in the situations wherein it is produced *as* it is being produced, attending expressly to the details of the situation and to events that perturb it. Any other form of observation, Garfinkel charges, *loses the phenomenon*. Thus the ethnomethodologist's researches limit themselves to direct observation, insert the researcher firmly into the situations under study, and often make use of cameras or other recording devices allowing the most minute details of the interactional sequence to be precisely recorded and closely examined. Understandably, this position awakens intense reactions among sociologists—and turns those adopting it into something of a sect within the discipline. But Garfinkel goes further. He finds even direct observation insufficient, if this is intended, at the end of the study, to produce observations viewed as valid in the judgment of an audience (for instance, other sociologists) found outside the situation under study. The result, he argues, can be but one more account among others, which cannot claim any particular validity in the eyes of the researcher or his audience.

When does a researcher find it possible to say in good conscience that he has produced an adequate understanding of the methods adopted within a given context in order to produce its social order? According to Garfinkel, the only plausible response to this query is—once again—processual and interactional. The researcher will have adequately understood the context he studies only after he has become a competent member in the situation, acknowledged as such by the other participants. On this account, ethnomethodological inquiries always require lengthy and laborious research efforts. For years, some practitioners have been induced to enroll in graduate studies of other disciplines, attending doctoral courses in mathematics or law (and earning a degree); or to live in a Tibetan monastery for so long that they were asked, in the end, to take part in sophisticated doctrinal debate; or to become professional truck drivers much appreciated as practitioners of that trade.

The ethnomethodological position has influenced the findings of the research it has authorized. Instead of explaining a phenomenon or a situation by appealing to abstract criteria (such as the bearing of the findings on the nature of the discipline) or to criteria extraneous to the situation itself (for instance, the intentions of those sponsoring and founding the research or the scientific community), Garfinkel has emphasized more and more the ability of research to produce *hybrid* materials, intended to invite the interested reader to enter into the situation studied by the researcher.

In Garfinkel's judgment, because the research is completed only after the researcher has successfully become a competent participant in a given situation, the account of the research is acceptable just to the extent that novices (or other participants in the situation) can employ it to develop and improve their own competence. Garfinkel labels such an outcome the *practical validity* of the research. Therefore, ethnomethodologists aim to produce what they call hybrid studies, texts (or other products) relevant both for the researchers who adopt the ethnomethodological perspective and for the very people who participate in the situations being analyzed. Perhaps this aspiration reveals a political ambition implicit in Garfinkel's research: to reconceptualize the nature of the social sciences in a way that allows them to consider the world anew, emphasizing the ordinary competence of concrete actors against the hubris of experts intent on formalizing reality and intervening with their techniques, instead of focusing the research effort on local and transitory situations and not procedures worked out from the outside and demanding universal application.

REFERENCES

Garfinkel, Harold, *The Perception of the Other: A Study in Social Order*, Ph.D. dissertation, Harvard University, 1952.

9 NIKLAS LUHMANN

German sociologist (1927–1998). After studying law and having a successful career as a civil servant, he developed an interest in sociological theory. He spent 1960–61 at Harvard University and in subsequent years pursued a career as an academic sociologist in Germany, receiving a chair in sociology at the University of Bielefeld. His early work primarily concerned organization and administrative studies. After his career change, Luhmann wrote an astonishing number of papers and books, devoted single-mindedly to developing his innovative (and controversial) version of social systems theory.

SUGGESTED READINGS
The Differentiation of Society, Columbia University Press, New York, 1982.
Social Systems, Stanford University Press, Palo Alto, California, 1995.
Ecological Communication, Chicago University Press, Chicago, 1989.
Observations on Modernity, Stanford University Press, 1998.

L UHMANN IS KNOWN in the Anglo-Saxon world as a radical antihumanist thinker, a theorist who sharply separates human actors—whom he calls *psychic systems*—from social systems. He is a sociologist with a reputation especially for being highly suspicious of any potential standard that may permit a societal critique from the standpoint of political or moral values.

Even though these assumptions may be, if properly qualified, correct, they do not imply that Luhmann's theories are not grounded in an explicit and systematically argued philosophical anthropology. On the contrary, he may be seen as the heir to a long-standing German philosophical tradition, rooted in the Enlightenment as well as in Romantic reactions to it. A main premise underlying his arguments is what we may call, introductorily, a *negative* anthropology. His main anthropological stance is that human beings are animals that do *not* have a biological determination; the main feature of the species, in comparison to other animals, is actually *not* having—or having many fewer—fixed biological mechanisms effectively restricting the range of perceptions, desires, and behaviors that may be carried out by individuals. As a result, humans have no automatic connection with their natural and social environment; they must discover and selectively establish some knowledge of it. For Bud Abbott, to determine that Lou Costello belongs to the human species tells him precious little of what Lou needs, wants, means, or does (and vice versa). This lack of determination makes many astonishing things possible, such as learning and self-determination. It also imposes a fundamental burden on all humans: they are at constant risk of being overwhelmed by the sheer complexity of what may happen next, which selections will be made, which habits and routines will eventually become taken for granted. Moreover, such utter complexity is not only external but also internal. Being underdetermined, human beings are constantly overburdened by what they may want, disdain, desire, strive for, or detest. To lead any sort of meaningful life, human beings must sharply reduce such potential complexity, relying on a range of mechanisms that exonerate (philologically speaking, *unburden*) them from facing it head-on.

Human beings need to select from many possibilities what they have to perceive, desire, think about, or act on. The contents of these selections—and whether they are (or are not) fair, efficient, adaptive, optimizing, moral, and so on—may be an important issue for any participant. Still, Luhmann believes that such concerns are largely secondary compared to the main functional need of reducing the complexity of the world to a manageable and meaningful level. No matter how dissatisfied I am with my boss, the last thing I want is to be suddenly drawn into a Mad Hatter tea party in the office supply closet while a horde of alien Greys raids my desk and my bank account, suddenly converting my savings into Cambodian riels.

According to Luhmann's anthropological stance, social complexity is reduced by two means. *Consciousness* provides a primary mechanism for complexity reduction. This is the result of our mind introducing a systematic gap between the external environment—that is, whatever structure or event constitutes a problem for the actor—and the internal universe of perception, feelings, drives, and desires. The existence of such a gap implies the possibility of temporal delay between perception and reaction, thus allowing *selection*, triage, reflective choice, or sheer avoidance. Through their internal processes, actors reduce complexity in many ways. First, they selectively schematize certain (and only certain) features of the environment, relegating anything else to the background. Lacking any biological determination, this largely subconscious selectivity is arbitrary (by any external observer's standpoint), and it may often turn out to be dangerous or suboptimal. Still, so long as it continues, this selective schematization places the actor in a situation where thinking is not overburdened by the complexity of the world. Subsequently, actors employ values, goals, objectives, and responsibility imputation (as well as many other stratagems) to further simplify the complexity of the issues they face, to select among them and justify to others the selections made. If I do not like spicy food, I can easily reduce the number of potential restaurant choices or simply skip all entrees marked in red.

Selection through consciousness, however, is not enough. Humans have strong, though limited, information-processing capacities and attention span. At the same time, the set of potential contingent events (what Luhmann calls *the horizon*) is awe-inspiring. Here is where social systems step in as extremely powerful mechanisms for complexity reduction. They reduce complexity by establishing a durable gap between the horizon of all possible communication and the (relatively) manageable, meaningful, actual communication deemed relevant by participants at a single moment in time and space. Social systems filter a limited amount of alternatives, successfully excluding others that could, if the selection process operated differently, well be selected. Social actors rely on the fact that other actors have or may make a large number of selections. Through social systems, their selections are transferred to others through various forms of communication, thus sharply reducing the complexity to be processed by the individual mind. Social systems, moreover, transfer these selections in ways that ensure a large number of them will be accepted, without the need for detailed schematization. Language is a great resource in this regard. But Luhmann also stresses the importance of what he calls *symbolically generalized communication media*, such as money, power, love, and truth. The fact that some goods are extremely expensive dramatically reduces the complexity of my shopping, and the equally complex ritual of human mating in contemporary society is highly facilitated by the unpleasant fact that many potential partners simply do not love us back.

SOCIAL SYSTEMS, PSYCHIC SYSTEMS

Luhmann's negative philosophical anthropology has some consequences for what is traditionally called "human freedom." Luhmann does not deny that such freedom exists; indeed, actors in similar situations may actually behave in sharply divergent ways. After all, the key proposition of his theory is that everything may be different and that social life is thus *contingent* (neither necessary nor random). But he is doubtful whether such freedom can be governed by a set of absolute ends that individuals are supposed to pursue, or by assuming that some social identities predefine individual selections. For Luhmann, freedom—from the individual's point of view—simply underscores the fact that whatever communication (action, values, norms, strategy, or preference) is chosen is always one possibility among others.

Individuals, as individuals, can be highly unpredictable; nobody really knows what is taking place in their minds. They can act and react in an astonishing variety of ways, many of which may surprise an observer. They may fail to notice interesting opportunities, deeply deceive themselves, and be systematically inconsistent at certain times and neurotically rigid at others; or they may act against their best interest. They may suddenly discover a passion for James Joyce, or equally unexpectedly for Lady Gaga. Even if they behave as expected, you never really know why they are doing so—or how long it will last. Precisely because they are autonomous and operate through consciousness, actors and their intentions are simply impenetrable to any social observation (short of those devices imagined in sci-fi novels). This makes it impossible to build a theory of social life on any *positive* anthropological foundation; it is simply not feasible to identify in good faith a stable core of needs, values, and preferences defining the individual as individual (and thus making it possible to assess how much society is able to respect her humanity).

Luhmann limits himself to stressing that individual freedom implies, from the point of view of a participant in communicative interaction, an ever-present margin of unpredictability. As we have already seen with Parsons, the social actor's potential unpredictability implies a continuous problem of stabilizing social expectations within a turbulent environment. To do so, social systems create a selective "island of lower complexity," governed by specific symbolic and operational structures that prioritize certain communication (effectively filtering out a large part of all possible communication). The more complex the environment, the more radical the selectivity put into operation by social systems must be. The larger the supply of available food in an economy, the more I need a supermarket that carefully selects its products.

What constitutes the relations between actors and social systems? Luhmann actually accepts a vision of human beings that grants them consciousness, intentionality, and autonomy, exactly as the classical European tradition (what he calls *old-European thinking*) has claimed since time immemorial. Once, Luhmann even argued that his theory could bear the title *Taking Individuals Seriously*. The difference is that, precisely because humans have consciousness and intentionality, there is no way to build a satisfactory theory of social life based on humanist premises. Just because they have intentionality and consciousness, Luhmann argues, social systems are never a component of any psychic system, as Durkheim imagined in his notion of *homo duplex*. Psychic systems, or minds, are operationally closed; they selectively perceive what takes place in their environment only so long as it is consistent with their own operations. Just a small fraction of the social environment may be actually perceived as significant by conscious individuals and acquire relevance for their thinking. In the same vein, from an observer's standpoint, the actual intentions of a participant are never known; they are sealed in the person's consciousness. Indeed, many disgustingly self-interested people perceive themselves as generous benefactors. Yet how creative they are in observing the consequences of their actions and experiences in ways that confirm such a self-perception!

At the same time, social systems are *not* mental operations in any way, as actual communication is equally sealed off from the mental state of the participant. Mental operations trigger events having potential communicative relevance (*utterances*), but they do not coincide with them. Mental operations do not determine if their informative potential will become actualized; nor can they predict its significance and subsequent developments. Nor too do participants' utterances reflect an "original" or "authentic" meaning. As many poets have observed, there is simply no way to fully express mental operations in communication, and any attempt by an actor to be fully transparent is at best self-defeating, or at worst deceitful. Communication assumes speakers have some kind of communicative intention; such intentions, however, are not derived from the content of the speaker's consciousness, but rather imputed to her. How many times have we tried to speak our mind, only to end up, like the ladies in T. S. Eliot's Prufrock, repeating endlessly "That is not it at all, that is not what I meant, at all"?

According to Luhmann, psychic systems are made only of those mental operations that selectively link themselves to previous mental operations and pose the conditions for further, equally selective rounds of thinking. Social systems, on the contrary, operate only through communication (related to previous communication), establishing the conditions for further communicative processes. The two systems are reciprocally sealed, each treating the other as part of its environment (this property is called by Luhmann *autopoiesis*).

MEANING, CONSCIOUSNESS, AND COMMUNICATION

Let's go deeper into the implication of such reciprocal "sealing" to better understand the similarities and differences between psychic and social systems.

Both systems are based on meaning (*Sinn*, sometimes also translated as *sense*, as in the expression "making sense"). But what is meaning? Luhmann offers a simple answer: it's the difference between what is actualized and the wide, potentially infinite horizons of possibilities that are not selected. The meaning of one relationship is given by the fact that we do not have as a partner somebody else; the meaning of a career is given by the many other activities we might have done for a living; the meaning of a classical drawing is its lack of baroque details; the meaning of a telephone call to our mother—regardless of the content—is showing that we care.

Both social and psychic systems are constituted by meaning precisely because they operate through selections; they "make sense" of the fact that something that could have happened actually occurred (or should have occurred) in a certain way. Social and psychic systems, moreover, must also deal with the same problem; the selection is never definitive and stable. The personal relationship we have entered into, no matter how strongly persuaded we may be or how satisfied we are, could sour or be challenged by new encounters. A career may fail or take an unexpected turn; a new understanding of the art world may conflate classical and baroque styles in the same artistic category. Every time this happens, the meaning of the situation changes in reference not only to the present but also to the past ("I was not really in love with him") or to the future ("What I really want is to go into marketing"). Eventually, both psychic and social systems are what Luhmann calls *observing systems*, entities that actively react to what they *perceive* as differences in their environment ("He is taking me for granted"; "Customers nowadays want shorter movies").

These similarities, however, do not imply that social systems are some kind of pseudo-human beings. They are actually two completely different species. Although they are both based on meaning, they process it differently; psychic systems, according to Luhmann, construct meaning through consciousness, inserting every event into a sequence linked to bodily feeling. We become conscious of the importance of somebody by the feeling of sadness that overcomes us when we hear she has died. Social systems process the "same" event in a wholly different way, inserting it into a sequence involving the other people's diverse understandings of the event and interpreting it according to various significance criteria. For a social system, someone's death is an environmental difference that may or may not become information according to the understanding of other actors. Like Garfinkel, Luhmann assumes that the actual social meaning of an utterance is not intrinsic to it; rather, it is contingently accomplished by the sequence of its reception on the part of the listeners. In our case, her death had to be "announced," becoming part of the potentially relevant information horizon. Subsequently, such information has to be understood by somebody else, in other words, selected as significant and processed through the code of a given social system (a potential new house listing for the real estate agent, a change in the payment schedule for the personnel office of an organization, an occasion of religious reflection for the faithful, a potential news item for the journalist, and so on). These understandings are independent—indeed, they may appear even disgusting—from the point of view and the feelings of the actor that gave the sad news. They also have ramifications in the form of further sequences of communication, provided these understandings are taken in turn as utterances with an informative value by other communications.

It is important to stress here that Luhmann does not restrict his analysis to linguistic statements. We communicate with money, actions, and involuntary behavior such as sneezing. I communicate even when I am not interested in communicating. When I walk into the supermarket to buy dinner, I am not particularly interested in communicating. Still, it is likely that a camera is actually observing my walking through the aisles, counting the minutes I am spending selecting groceries and reporting the outcome to some marketing employee who will understand such information in terms of my willingness to pay more for organic asparagus if they are placed in a well-lit corner 1.45 meters from the floor. Such understanding on the part of the marketing employee may feed into further rounds of communications to farmers, furniture designers, packaging factories, and many other actors who will understand it according to their strategies, thus creating further rounds of communication that will keep, together with myriad others, the economic system "alive."

We may further explore this example to better clarify what Luhmann means by communication. First, the fact that communication requires understanding does not imply that such understanding is "authentic," and even less that it follows the "intended" meaning of the action. On the basis of its understanding my buying the asparagus, the marketing department may launch an ad campaign so boring that I will actually stop buying asparagus. Or they will make the asparagus so overpriced that I will not be able to afford them. The impact of the campaign would then be some change in my shopping strategy: switching to another supermarket or to some other vegetable, or a reduction in my consumption of asparagus. Or I may fail to even notice the price increase. In all cases, these changes may become further differences, may be entrusted (or not) with informative potential, and may be understood in some way as significant by others. In short, for Luhmann what matters is not "correct" understanding that deciphers the intention of the emitter, nor generation of an "appropriate" response. Luhmann's requirement is that communication, like the proverbial show, must go on. From the point of view of social systems, "success" in communication is not compliance—no matter how strongly a psychic system may seek it—but simply the fact that it triggers further information utterances. Only interruption of communication may cause the death of a social system, exactly as irreversible interruption of consciousness implies the end of a psychic system.

Another important consideration is the fact that buying the asparagus is not an "economic" selection. Communications and actions do not belong to specific types or kinds. The same video recording used by the marketing department may be used by the police to investigate a crime, by an NGO interested in making a political claim on the consumers' willingness to go green, by a behavioral scientist interested in studying postures or clothing, or by a lawyer concerned with privacy rights abuses. In this case, the very same utterance (my buying the asparagus) will be coded differently (respectively in economic, legal, political, scientific, and legal terms), understood in light of varying premises giving rise to differentiated sequences of communication. All of them will be largely independent from my motivation to buy asparagus, or my intention to communicate something.

VARIETIES OF SOCIAL SYSTEMS

According to Luhmann, reduction of complexity occurs throughout all systems. As well, social systems are based on meaning, which is processed by communication. Social systems treat psychic systems as part of their environment, but importantly, not all social systems are the same. Luhmann distinguishes among three species, each treating the others as elements in their respective environment.

Interactions are based on the physical co-presence of participants who perceive the presence of others. Here, closely following Goffman and Garfinkel, Luhmann assumes that co-presence automatically generates social systems, as no participant may actually refuse to communicate without generating some communication about her refusal. The survival of systems of this kind is contingent on physical co-presence, or in the contemporary area of electronic communication on to-kens or avatars that are its functional equivalent. Interaction reduces complexity through sharp limitation of the number of participants (we can have a conver-sation with only a handful of people at once), enabling discussion of a limited number of issues ("Would you stop jumping from one issue to another?") with local references ("I am just not interested in your aunt from Kansas"), taking all other—surrounding—communication as a given or as "noise" ("Are you *really* listening to the people at the other table instead of listening to me?").

Societies are encompassing systems whose boundaries coincide with the boundaries of communication. Luhmann endlessly stresses that societies are not coterminous with states or geographical portions of territory, let alone with "cultures." Since modern times, there exists one single society, a "world society," spanning the globe. The subdivision of territories into nation states is only a segmental differentiation of the world society's political subsystem. Societies reduce complexity through differentiation, whether segregation of participants into smaller categories or establishment of specialized codes for selecting communication. As we will see shortly, it is possible to distinguish at least three subsequent forms of societal differentiation: segmented, stratified, and functionally differentiated (this last being what is usually called "modern" or "contemporary" society).

Organizations are social systems based on a formal definition of membership. Luhmann describes them as decision networks, presented in their communica-tion as related to formally prescribed rules. Organizations reduce complexity, absorbing uncertainty by treating it as a matter of choice for specific offices, thus making possible a set of relatively repeatable, stable activities that serve as refer-ents in case of disagreement regarding membership rules and formal positions. Latecomers in the history of social systems, they clearly did not exist in many forms of early societies and were largely marginal in others. Only in modern and contemporary society have they acquired an important role in structuring communication and reducing complexity.

Luhmann does not see the relationships among these three kinds of systems as a matter of level, such as micro (interactions), meso (organizations), and macro (society). Nor does he believe that interactions are the building blocks of organizations and organizations of society. He stresses sharply that they are three independent species of social systems, each treating the others as elements in its own environment.

As an example, let's say I go to work in a financial firm and I have a meeting with some colleagues to discuss the consequences for the security market of what has recently happened (we have just discovered from the Internet) in Mongolia. Concurrently, we work for an organization, we participate in an interaction, and through our talking and using the Internet we reproduce the societal network of communication. This does not imply there are three sequences of communication taking place simultaneously. On the contrary, the very same communication events are being processed by all three kinds of systems according to different significance criteria, with each system drawing a boundary between what is significant and what is not.

THE EVOLUTION OF SOCIAL SYSTEMS

The co-presence of all three kinds of social systems in modern society does not imply that their structural relationships have always been the same. On the contrary, their relationship has evolved remarkably throughout the history of the human species. Early hominids—and for a long time, *Homo sapiens sapiens* too—lived in small societies with an endemic tendency toward frequent personal contact. In their case, society and interaction largely coincided, and personal experience and long-term habits could be successfully used to stabilize communication through tradition-backed, shared expectations. These societies differentiated only *segmentally*. Whenever the number of members exceeded the capacity for a system of interaction to regulate communication, they split into roughly similar independent groups.

Some of the segmented groups subsequently experienced an evolutionary differentiation of interaction and society through emergence of two means for introducing a difference—and thus a system-environment distinction—within itself. Some societies distinguished between a center and the periphery, between a space of intense communication and more sparsely populated areas from which communications may flow only through a restricted number of nodes. Others evolved into what Luhmann calls *stratified* societies. Here the distinction differentiates strata, castes, and status groups, with each treating the others as elements of its environment.

Luhmann uses the term *stratification* differently from contemporary social stratification research; the latter refers in its important studies to the location of *individuals* in reference to the degree of access to important social resources (wealth, income, education, power, consumption, and so on), while Luhmann refers instead to differentiation of societies into unequal subsystems, defined by restrictions on the significance of communication across their boundaries.

Stratified societies accommodate a much larger network of communication, reducing complexity through segregation of participants into largely impermeable strata. Among the strata, there are wide differences in terms of wealth, power, and prestige. From Luhmann's point of view, however, such inequalities are not significant in and by themselves, but for the consequences they have for communication. System stratification reduces the number of participants and establishes a clear, *ex-ante*, asymmetrical significance of communication according to their location in the various strata. There is a pecking order among strata, with each treating those below as components of the environment, often in roughly similar forms to those employed for animals and objects (think about Aristotle's statement, "The slave is a living tool and the tool a lifeless slave"). The upper stratum functions as an independent society, and the communications originating from it are classified *ex-ante* as significant, while the opposite is true for peasants (unless you are Joan of Arc). To use Luhmann's wording, the highest stratum "represents society within society." Luhmann also stresses that the lower classes in a stratified society suffer not just from lack of provisions and entitlements; they also face extreme difficulty in participating in any kind of influential communication, such that their only option is often to engage in riots, uprisings, or millenarian movements. The case of Joan of Arc demonstrates how these are all risky and costly attempts at such communication.

The form of societal differentiation Luhmann is most interested in, unsurprisingly, is the functional one embodied in modern society. Its emergence is rooted in a single space and time: Western Europe between the 16th and 17th centuries. His basic idea is that modern society has started to organize communication through a variety of specialized systems, operating according to specific, independent, symbolic codes; leading values; operational programs; and regulative means:

The economy has become a specialized subsystem, dealing with the problem of securing future satisfaction of want.

Politics has become another, concerned with production of binding decisions.

Religion has retired into a specialized activity targeted on interpreting the incomprehensible.

A legal system, centered on securing maintenance of shared expectations in the face of possible disappointments, has emerged.

Science has differentiated as a form of communication oriented toward ascertaining verifiable facts.

The education system has specialized in trying to produce communication-adequate psychic systems, operating through the supply of generalized, graded individuals' certifications on which other subsystems and organizations may rely.

The mass media have emerged, specializing in generating a "present" operating throughout society and familiar to individuals.

Art has differentiated through its specialization in addressing the contingency of existing perception and symbolisms.

Contrary to Parsons, Luhmann does not believe there are a fixed number of subsystems entrusted with stable contributions to society. Luhmann's subsystems evolve by chance, in a kind of natural evolution, becoming institutionalized through introduction of functional codes that effectively filter the communication in a specific way. In fact, Luhmann argues, in contemporary society everything that happens may be processed by law in terms of being lawful or unlawful, by the economy in terms of having or not having the possibility to pay, by religion in terms of immanence or transcendence, by art in terms of beautiful or ugly, by science as true or false, by education in terms of "transmissible" or "nontransmissible." Although Parsons assumed one subsystem was specialized in the integration of society, Luhmann asserts that in a functionally differentiated society nothing keeps all these systems together

in any particular way, and none of them may claim any kind of special, ordering, or superordinate status. Very simply, each system treats the rest of society
as its environment.

THE CHALLENGES OF A DIFFERENTIATED
SOCIETY AND THE DANGERS OF MORALITY

A large portion of Luhmann's writings is devoted to exploring the implications of
the functional differentiation of contemporary society. First, being functionally
differentiated, contemporary society has no head, no base, and no center. Some
empirical asymmetries may be registered, but there is no possibility of structural determination, even in the last instance. All systems are at the same time
autonomous and heavily constrained by (what they perceive as) the externalities
of other subsystems. Politicians may try to steer the economy through regulation
and taxation, while entrepreneurs may try to influence politics through protest,
lobbying, or corruption. To do so, however, they must operate within the code
of their own subsystem: politicians must use power and entrepreneurs must
use money. Politicians will interpret the use of money by entrepreneurs in political terms, while entrepreneurs will observe if the political decisions enacted
have implications for making or losing money. This applies to any interaction
between differentiated subsystems; each of them filters what happens according
to its own specific and incommensurable code. For example, judicial cases increasingly rely on scientifically certified evidence to adjudicate claims. Still, to be
legally valid, such evidence must have been lawfully obtained and analyzed, and
even so, jurors with no scientific credentials may decide to largely disregard it if
they want. At the same time, there is no doubt that the legal system often inter-
feres with scientific research, banning some kinds of experiments and imposing
certain precautionary procedures, or requesting informed consent for a growing
number of research studies. Still, judges cannot adjudicate scientific controversy;
nor can they establish what is scientifically true. They can only jail the scientists.

Another implication Luhmann often stresses is that in a differentiated society it is simply impossible to steer or control a subsystem from the outside. Each
subsystem may try to do so (what Luhmann calls *irritating*), but all others will
interpret the consequences of such irritation according to their own codes and
programs. If the state tries to implement certain procedures for selecting personnel, such measures will be interpreted not according to the spirit of the law

but rather according to the difference they might make for profitability and for the organizational routines of firms. In effect, the law may trigger fairer access to jobs for certain groups. But it may just as well result in processes of outsourcing, greater use of subcontracting, shifting to other sectors of the economy—in other words, it may activate other processes that run counter to the intentions of the legislators.

There is simply no central authority to steer society along a certain course, no matter how beneficial this may appear. The point is particularly evident in Luhmann's analysis of the global environmental situation. He takes quite seriously the scientific evidence pointing to the planet's resources being stretched to the limit. At the same time, no functional subsystem can be entrusted with solving the problem, and there is no way in which any one of them can regulate the others in order to plan a more sustainable course. In contemporary society, there are only subsystems observing each other and reacting to the consequences of their activities selectively, through an interpretation based on their own specialized function. Luhmann documents how the problem of the environment is not the outcome of the operation of a single system, but rather of the complex combination of the externalities of all of them. Each subsystem, however, deals only selectively with the changes in the natural environment and according to its own code. There is simply no means to coordinate such specialized interpretations consistently. The capacity to influence what is happening is consequently limited, and the outcome of any political or legal measure will be determined not on its own terms but by how all other systems will react to such irritation.

Another important implication of functional differentiation, also having worrisome consequences, is that such a society has no predefined role for the individual, no generalized criteria to prescribe the "good life," and no special social relationship on which the status of the person may be thought to depend. Contrary to previous forms of differentiation, which attributed to the individual a master status (usually through the household he or she belonged to), functionally differentiated societies have no room for the "person." From the point of view of society, each individual is an uncoordinated bundle of communicative positions that a subsystem interprets according to its specialized code. Here individuals do not have assigned seats; they are dissolved into myriad specialized communications traversing a hall of echo chambers.

The "brighter" side of functionally differentiated societies is that, in contrast to stratified societies, they do not *have to* operate through systematic exclusion. As functional systems operate according to differentiated codes, they do not exclude anybody *as a matter of principle*. Everyone is included or excluded in various ways within different subsystems, according to his or her control of the means of communication pertinent to each single subsystem. All those with money (regardless of how little) can participate in the economy, and even the most prejudiced seller is forced by the market economy to sell her wares to whoever is willing to buy them. The pedagogically minded assume that everybody can (and should) be educated. Politicians think that everyone can (and should) participate in political life, and any scribble on the wall may be appreciated as art or despised according to its aesthetic qualities. In a differentiated society, communication discriminates according to the code of the subsystem, not according to the ascribed master status of the individual. Does Luhmann really believe this is the actual condition of contemporary society? Not exactly, and he has never claimed so. On the contrary, a major goal of his analysis of social evolution is precisely to stress some critical consequences of functional differentiation for the inclusion of individuals and populations.

First, in his theory, each form of differentiation displaces (but does not eliminate) the previous forms of differentiation. Stratified societies had an important segmental dimension (family lineage) and reflected several center-periphery cleavages. In the same way, contemporary society is *primarily* a functionally differentiated society, but stratification, center-periphery cleavage, and segmental differentiation all play an important role. It is not only that specialized subsystems have to deal with the legacy of the previous inequalities. It is also that these secondary forms of differentiation are often quite handy for subsystem-specific activities. Entrepreneurs, operating fully within a differentiated economic code, routinely segment their customer base according to regional or class position if this implies a chance of higher profit. Politicians, operating with yet another fully differentiated political code, may still find many of these cleavages useful, as the wealth of regionalist, ethnic, and lifestyle political organizations documents. The primacy of functional differentiation implies that previous forms of differentiation are used—reproduced and even strengthened—*functionally*, not that they are obliterated or repressed.

Luhmann also acknowledges that although functional codes do not *need* to introduce forms of exclusion based on personal status to operate, they may still produce exclusion *factually*, through their own operation. Functional differentiation of the economic system, for example, has created an enormous, and still growing, gap between "developed" centers and "underdeveloped" peripheries throughout the world. Differentiation of the political system has greatly increased the range of possible binding decisions, including many that have been extremely violent or genocidal. Luhmann stresses that all functional subsystems "presuppose inclusion of every human being, but in fact they exclude persons not meeting their requirements" (Luhmann, 1997: 71). Because the failure to meet such requirements is often empirically interdependent, exclusion from one subsystem in many cases implies proliferation of exclusions from other spheres. If you live on one dollar or less per day, as a significant part of humanity does, economic-oriented communication will hardly even realize you are there, and the same applies to many other subsystems. Luhmann has repeatedly stressed that large numbers of human beings are factually excluded, unable to irritate any subsystem, and thus largely irrelevant and invisible to them. Luhmann thinks that blaming such situation on "inequality" or "exploitation" is inadequate. Although such a view may prompt important moral or political actions, it also obfuscates the fact that functional differentiation generates specific structural forms of *neglect*; very simply, anyone who cannot participate in specialized communication, regardless of the reason, simply disappears from the radar. Personal exclusion is functionally unnecessary, but it is nevertheless ironclad. Even the mass media require an ever-higher number of gory deaths in covering the global excluded. The problem, claims Luhmann, is not that certain politicians or entrepreneurs are evil. The problem is that such radical exclusion—such *reduction of persons to bodies*, as he defines it—may turn out to be part and parcel of functional differentiation itself. As with the ecological problem, Luhmann finds out that no functional subsystem can regulate the others in order to plan a more inclusive course; nor is there a central point from which it is possible to voice (and to have heard) claims for inclusion. As he writes:

The worst imaginable scenario might be that the society of the next century will have to accept the metacode of inclusion/exclusion. And this would mean that some human beings will be persons and others only individuals; that some are included into function systems for (successful or unsuccessful) careers and others are excluded from these systems, remaining bodies that try to survive the next day; that some are emancipated as persons and others are emancipated as bodies; that concern and neglect become differentiated along this boundary; that tight coupling of exclusions and loose couplings of inclusions differentiate fate and fortune; and that two forms of integration will compete: the negative integration of exclusions and the positive integration of inclusions [Luhmann, 1997: 77].

Luhmann identifies a third problem, deriving from the fact that, once functional differentiation becomes the primary form of reproduction of the system-environment distinction within society, there is no guarantee that the operations of the subsystems will remain compatible with one another. The mass-media-differentiated operation may cause a large decline in political trust, medical research may cause disastrous demographic consequences, romantic love may become a problem in the workplace and so affect the careers of individuals, the strength of legal regimes blocks the exercise of political power, and artistic production may undermine values necessary for economic production. As for environment and inclusion, society evolves, but it cannot control where its evolution leads. To put it bluntly, Luhmann believes we must acknowledge that, given the absence of any center that can coordinate subsystems, the only thing that may be said about their future compatibility is that it will last as long as it will last.

Luhmann is neither optimistic about the future of contemporary society nor complacent about the amount of risk, danger, and suffering it produces. Within this context, it is possible to better qualify the criticism mentioned in the beginning of this chapter, of Luhmann as a skeptical theorist willing to despise any moral project. Luhmann does not deny that morality matters, and he is even willing to recognize that in contemporary societies there is an endemic and widespread diffusion of moral concerns. In our society, where we cannot settle all issues according to some unproblematic tradition, actors constantly face moral issues, from voting to recycling. Bud Abbott is not only worried about the morality of Lou Costello but also concerned about his own morality. What characterizes Luhmann's approach is rather keen attention to the limits of political will and the acknowledgment that moral discourses cannot be considered as external to communication; nor can they claim a status higher than other ways of selecting among possibilities. He writes that morality, from a sociological point of view, is simply "the symbolic generalization that reduces the full reflexive complexity of doubly contingent ego / alters relations to expressions of esteem" (Luhmann,

1996: 236). Although there is no reason to deny it may have important, and sometimes positive, consequences (I will walk further to bring my old newspapers to the recycling bin), there is no reason to claim that such consequences are more important or straightforward than those that may be used to induce me to do so, such as money (I will walk longer to bring my old newspapers because I can sell them there), power (if they discover my old newspapers in the ordinary garbage, they will give me a fine), or love (she is so keen on recycling my newspapers!). Attempts to solve the complex problems of a functionally differentiated society through simplified judgments of esteem and disdain, he warns, risk being not only ineffective but also dangerous. As Luhmann stresses, "Moralists are contentious people" (Luhmann, 1984: 17).

REFERENCES

Luhmann, Niklas, 1984, I fondamenti sociali della morale, *Fenomenologia e società*, 1984, 7(1), 5–37.

Luhmann, *Social Systems*, Stanford University Press, Palo Alto, California, 1996.

Luhmann, Globalization or world society? How to conceive of modern society, *International Review of Sociology*, 1997, 7(1), 67–80.

OTHER WAYS

OF ENCOUNTERING

THE SAME AUTHORS

Ours is not the only way to approach these authors. Other scholars have chosen other paths, with valuable results.

Some have treated more than one of our authors, together with still more thinkers we have not ourselves considered here.

Alexander, Jeffrey C. *Theoretical Logic in Sociology* (4 vols.). Berkeley: University of California Press, 1982–83.

———. *Twenty Lectures: Sociological Theory Since World War Two*. New York: Columbia University Press, 1987.

Aron, Raymond. *Main Currents in Sociological Thought*. Garden City, New York: Anchor Books, 1968–1970.

Collins, Randall. *Four Sociological Traditions*. New York: Oxford University Press, 1994.

Coser, Lewis. *Masters of Sociological Thought: Ideas in Historical and Social Context*. Orlando, Florida: Harcourt Brace Jovanovich, 1977.

Giddens, Anthony. *Capitalism and Modern Social Theory: An Analysis of the Writings of Marx, Durkheim and Max Weber*. Cambridge, UK: Cambridge University Press, 1971.

Joas, Hans, and Wolfgang Knoebl. *Social Theory: Twenty Introductory Lectures*. Cambridge University Press, 2009.

Some others have published significant works containing authoritative discussions of one or the other of authors to whom we have devoted a chapter.

Burns, Tom. *Erving Goffman*. New York: Routledge, 1991.

Frisby, David. *Georg Simmel*. London: Tavistock, 1984.

Heritage. John. *Garfinkel and Ethnomethodology*. London: Polity, 1991.

Joas, Hans. *G. H. Mead: A Contemporary Re-examination of His Thought*. Cambridge, Mass.: MIT Press, 1997.

Kaesler, Dirk. *Max Weber: An Introduction to His Life and Work* (transl. Philippa Hurd). Chicago: University of Chicago Press, 1988.

Lukes, Steven. *Emile Durkheim, His Life and Work: A Historical and Critical Study.* Palo Alto, Calif.: Stanford University Press, 1985.

McLellan, David. *The Thought of Karl Marx: An Introduction.* London: Macmillan, 1980.

Moeller, Hans-Georg. *Luhmann Explained: From Souls to Systems.* Chicago: Open Court, 2006.

Wearne, Bruce. *The Theory and Scholarship of Talcott Parsons to 1951: A Critical Commentary.* Cambridge: Cambridge University Press, 2009.

Last but not least, others have provided edited volumes with a selection of the writings of some of these thinkers.

Bellah, Robert N. *Emile Durkheim on Morality and Society.* Chicago: Chicago University Press, 1973.

Lemert, Charles, and Ann Branaman. *The Goffman Reader.* Hoboken, N. J.: Wiley-Blackwell, 1997.

Levine, Donald N. *Georg Simmel on Individuality and Social Forms.* Chicago: University of Chicago Press, 1972.

McLellan, David. *Karl Marx: Selected Writings.* Oxford: Oxford University Press, 2000.

Strauss, Anselm (ed.). *George Herbert Mead: On Social Psychology.* Chicago: University of Chicago Press, 1964.

Turner, Bryan S. *The Talcott Parsons Reader.* Hoboken, N. J.: Wiley-Blackwell, 1991.

Wright Mills, Charles, and Hans Geerth. *From Max Weber: Essays in Sociology.* Oxford: Oxford University Press, 1958.

INDEX

Action theory, 105

Aesthetic dimension of social life, 11, 20, 52, 73–74, 78

AGIL model, 112–16

Alienation: Marx on, 20, 21–22; Simmel on, 87–89. *See also* Anomy

Anomy, 36–38, 47, 48. *See also* Suicide, anomic

Anthropology, negative vs. positive, 155, 157–8

Aristotle, 7, 165

Art, 13, 114, 166

Atomism (Parsons), 106–107

Autonomy: Parsons on, 106–107, 109

Autopoiesis, 160

Base (Marx), 11–12

Blasé attitude, 88–89

Bourdieu, Pierre, 4

Bourgeoisie, 16, 19, 29, 21–23, 35, 60–61. *See also* Classes

Bureaucracy, 65–8

Calvin/ism, 62–63

Capitalism, rise of: Marx on 17–18; Weber on, 60–64. *See also* Production, capitalist mode of

Capitalism, unsustainability of (Marx), 23–26

Class conflict/struggle, 20, 22–24, 25, 36, 57–58, 60

Classes: Marx on, 9–10, 16; Weber on, 57–58. *See also* Bourgeoisie; Class conflict/ struggle; Proletariat

Classics, sociological, 2–4

Canon, sociological, 3, 4

Charismatic leadership: Weber on, 68

Citizenship, 119–120

Collective Representations, 32–33, 38–39

Commodities, 16–18, 24

Communication: Luhmann on 161–2, 163–4, 165; Mead on, 97–98, 104

Complexity, reduction of (Luhmann), 156–7, 162

Consciousness: Luhmann on, 156–7, 160–161; Simmel on, 92–95

Corporations (Durkheim), 36

Creative destruction (Marx), 18

Division of Labor (Durkheim), 31–35, 42

Documentary method of interpretation (Garfinkel), 145

Double contingency (Parsons), 108

Dramaturgical performance. *See* Presentation of Self

Durkheim, Emile, 4, 27–48, 84, 98, 159; as reformist, 48. Works: *Division of Labor in Society, The*, 31; *Elementary Forms of Religious Life, The*, 45, 47, 84; *Leçons sociologie* (*Professional Ethics and Civic Morals*), 35; *Rules of the Sociological Method, The*, 29–30; *Suicide*, 37–38, 38–39

Economy: Durkheim on, 36–37, 42–43; Luhmann on 161–2, 166, 168, 169–70; Parsons on, 111, 114–15, 117, 118; Simmel on, 75, 80–86; Weber on 52–53, 58–60, 60–64

Education, 11, 18, 114, 165, 166

Egoism: Durkheim on, 47–48

Engels, Friedrich, 7, 22, 25

Enlightenment, 46, 155

Ethnomethodology, 137, 145, 150–53

Exploitation, 13–14, 15, 20, 21–22, 60, 170

Family, 11, 20, 42, 78, 81, 114
Fashion: Simmel on, 72
Foucault, Michel, 4
Frames (Goffman), 132–3
Fundamentalism (Parsons), 115–16

Game (Simmel), 102
Garfinkel, Harold, 4, 137–53, 161, 163; and Agnes, 148–9; communication experiments of, 146–8
Generalized means of interchange. *See* Money, Parsons on
German philosophy, 8, 155
Generalization (Simmel), 98–100; and institutions, 99–100
Generalized other, 102–104
Gestures (Simmel), 100–101; conversations of, 97
Goffman, Erving, 4, 121–36, 163

Habermas, Jürgen, 4
Hegel, Georg, 21, 79, 87
Hirschman, Albert (*The Passions and the Interests*), 81
Historical change, Marx on, 12–15; Parsons on, 119–120; Weber on, 63–64
Homo duplex, 27–29, 34–35, 36–38, 38–39, 43–44, 46–47, 159
Homo faber, 7–8, 12
Human freedom (Luhmann), 157–8
Human mental life (Mead), 94–95
Human nature: Garfinkel on, 137–8, 142; Luhmann on, 155–7, 164; Mead on, 91; Simmel on, 71–72. *See also Homo duplex; Homo faber;* Humans
Humans: as interpretive beings (Weber), 49–51, 55–56, 59; as non–transparent (Goffman), 121–2; as normative (Parsons), 105–106

Individual motivations, perfect institutional integration of (Parsons), 111–12

Individualization: Durkheim on, 34–35, 37–38, 39–45, 47–48; Goffman on, 133–36; Luhmann on, 168; Simmel on 77–79; Weber on, 68–69
Industrialization: Marx on, 17–18, 23
Inequality, social: Goffman on, 130–132; Luhmann on, 169–71; multidimensional vs. one–dimensional vision of, 57; Parsons on, 119–20
Institutionalized individualism (Parsons), 107
Interaction, social, the nature of: actors' accounts of, 150–53; Garfinkel on, 141–49; Parsons on, 107–12, 116–19
Interaction order, the, 122, 127–28, 129–33, 135; civil inattention, 130; demeanor, 131–2; forgiveness, 130; open persons, 131–2; repair, 129–30, stigma 130–31
Ideal types, 51–55, 56–57
Interests: Durkheim on, 29, 32–38, 38–45; Marx on, 9–10, 10–15, 19–23, 24–25; Simmel on, 74–75, 81–82; Weber on, 51, 55, 58–59, 65–68
Intersubjectivity (Weber), 50

Kant, Immanuel, 71
Katascopic vs. anascopic perspective (Simmel vs. Durkheim), 84

Labor power, 14, 15–18, 21
Law/legal systems: Luhmann on, 166, 177; Marx on, 11, 13, 19; Parsons on, 115–16
Legitimacy of authority (Weber), 54–55, 65
Lenin, Vladimir, 7
Luhmann, Niklas, 4, 155–72
Luther, Martin (*Beruf*), 61–62

Marx, Karl, 4, 7–26, 27, 57–60, 63, 87, 118; "the economist," 21–22; political activities of, 20; "the young," 21, 22. Works: *Capital*, 22; *Communist Manifesto, The*, 22–23, 57; *German Ideology, The*, 25; *Grundriss, The* ("Forms Which Precede the Capitalist Mode of Production"), 14–15

Mead, George Herbert, 4, 91–104
Meaning: Garfinkel on, 137–41, 142–8;
    Luhmann on, 160–2; Mead on, 94–95,
    98–99; Weber on, 49–51, 55–60
Methodology, scientific: Weber on 56–57
Mobility, social: Parsons on, 119–20
Modernity/modernization: Durkheim on,
    31–38, 42–43; Luhmann on 164–7; Marx
    on; 14, 18–19; Parsons on, 113–16, 119–
    20; Simmel on, 78–79, 85–86; Weber
    on, 68–69
Money: and disengagement, 80–82, 85;
    Luhmann on, 157, 161, 167; Marx on,
    16–17, 20; Parsons on, 118–19; Simmel
    on 79–86, 88, 89
Morality: Luhmann on, 167–72
Morphological features of society, 31–33
Methodenstreit, 56

Norms: Durkheim on, 30, 36–38, 39, 43–45;
    Garfinkel on, 139–41, 143; Goffman on,
    129–31; Parsons on, 107–112; Weber on,
    50–51

Objective vs. subjective spirit (Simmel), 79

Parsons, Talcott, 4, 105–120, 140, 158, 166
Parties, political, 57–58, 67–68
Pathos (Durkheim), 43–45, 46–47
Philosophical anthropology, 1, 27, 49, 54, 59,
    134, 155, 157
Play (Simmel), 100–102
Power, political: Durkheim on, 35–37;
    Luhmann on, 166, 167; Marx on, 11, 13,
    18–19; Parsons on, 119; Weber on 58,
    64–69
Presentation of self, 123–9, 130–31;
    construction of self in, 126; definition
    of the situation in, 124; and "face," 125–
    6; and human communication, 123–4;
    and social actors, 124–6
Production (Marx), 8–10; capitalist mode
    of, 15–23; control over means of, 10–15;
    means of, 9; modes of, 14–15

Proletariat, 16, 20, 21–24. *See also* Classes
Public policy, 18–19

Rationality, value–based vs. instrumental,
    53–54
Religion: Durkheim on, 45–48; Luhmann
    on, 166; Marx on, 10–11, 13, 19–20, 58,
    59; Weber on 52, 58–60, 63–64. *See also*
    Spirit of capitalism; theodicy
Revolution: Marx on, 13, 15, 22, 23–26
Romanticism, 8, 155
Routine: Weber on, 54

Sacred vs. profane, 45–46
Sanctions: Durkheim on, 29–30, 35, 44;
    Parsons on, 116–19
Science, 13, 19–20, 24, 42–3, 52, 58, 69, 79,
    166, 167
Simmel, Georg, 4, 71–89, 118; and "cultural
    pessimism," 79, 86–87; as paradoxical
    72, 82. Works: "Concept and the
    Tragedy of Culture, The," 87; "Excursus
    on the 'Stranger,'" 72; "Metropolis
    in Mental Life, The," 87; *Philosophy
    of Money, The*, 79, 80; "Quantitative
    Aspects of the Group," 77; Soziologie,
    77; "Web of Group Affiliations, The"
    ("The Intersection of Social Circles"),
    77, 82
Smith, Adam, 2, 7, 80
Social facts, 29–30, 38, 44, 46
Socialization: Simmel on, 101–104
Solidarity, mechanical vs. organic, 33–35
Species evolution (Simmel), 95–98
Spirit of capitalism (Weber), 60–63
State, the: Weber on 55, 64–69
Status groups, 57–58
Suicide, 39–45; altruistic, 40–41; anomic,
    41–42, 48; egoistic, 40, 42; and "moral
    constitution," 39–40
Superstructure (Marx), 11–12
Symbolic interactionism, 91, 121
Symbolically generalized communication
    media. *See* Money, Luhmann on

Systems, Social: functional differentiation in, 167–72; irritation in, 167–68, 170; Luhmann on 157–72; and morality, 168, 171–72; and observing systems, 160; Parsons on, 112–119; and psychic systems, 155, 157–60, 162, 166; stratification in 164–65

Technology, 12, 14, 17, 19, 24, 25, 31, 36, 37, 42–43, 79, 88
Theodicy, 52
Total institution, 127; and amoral acts of shamelessness, 127; and territories of the self, 127
Totemism (Durkheim), 45

Unsociable sociability (Simmel), 71, 73–74, 75–76, 78, 80

Urban life, modern: Simmel on, 87–89
Utilitarian thought 32–34, 41, 44, 86

Values: Parsons on 110–11, 118
Vierkandt, Alfred, 77
von Wiese, Leopold, 77

Wealth of Nations, The, 80
Weber, Max, 4, 49–69. Works: "City, The," 53; Economy and Society, 53, 59; Protestant Ethic and the Spirit of Capitalism, The, 59, 63
Working class. See Proletariat; Classes; Class conflict/struggle

Zusammenbruch (total breakdown, collapse), 24–25